CW0819390

FULHAM'S GOLDEN YEARS

SUBSCRIPTION COPY

Number: 25

FULHAM'S GOLDEN YEARS

A Pictorial Memoir of Fulham Football Club
1958-1983

FULHAM'S GOLDEN YEARS

A Pictorial Memoir of Fulham Football Club
1958-1983

KEN COTON

ASHWATER
PUBLISHING

First published October 1992

Ashwater Publishing
68 Tranmere Road Whitton Twickenham Middlesex

© *Ken Coton*

ISBN 0 9515217 2 1

Printed by K & N Press, Molesey, Surrey
Bound by Fairfax Bookbinders, Fulham

FOREWORD

by Graham Leggat

I felt both flattered and honoured when asked to write a foreword to this pictorial review of Fulham's halcyon days. After all, I played alongside two of Fulham's most recognisable names—the then England skipper, Johnny Haynes, and the England manager-to-be, Bobby Robson. Nevertheless, I am delighted to recall some of the happy memories from my days at the Cottage, memories brought vividly back to mind by Ken Coton's wonderful collection of photographs.

It wouldn't be fair, I suppose, to name names, but I will anyway. There are four that I will always think of with more than the usual affection. They hardly feature in this book, but Frank Osborne, Beddy Jezzard, Frank Penn and Joe Bacuzzi—the back-room boys—for me, made Fulham Football Club something very special.

So special that, although I now live some 3,600 air miles from Stevenage Road, it's not difficult to let my mind drift back to the late Fifties and early Sixties at the Cottage... There was a sort of show-biz atmosphere about *our* Fulham, whether it was the likes of Tommy Trinder and Chappie D'Amato in the boardroom, or film stars like Honor Blackman, Michael Craig and Peter Vaughan in the stands, or perhaps characters like Tosh Chamberlain and Rodney Marsh on the pitch. The Cottage was a fun place.

I know we were regarded at times as a bit of a social club, perhaps a little short of ambition. After all, the annual Boat Race was one of the highlights of the season. And yes, we did have a better than average cricket team. And our golf team (which won the only trophy in the boardroom) was simply outstanding. Despite that, our football team, on its day, could more than hold its own with any First Division side.

If only it had been 'our day' more often!!

My biggest thrill with Fulham (apart from gaining promotion in my first season) was also my biggest disappointment—the semi-final matches against Burnley in 1962. Burnley had a very talented side, but we could and should have won. Had we reached Wembley, I am convinced we would have beaten Spurs. But it wasn't to be.

I must be honest, I miss: the silky smooth left foot of Eddie Lowe; the challenge of putting my head in the path of a Tosh Chamberlain cross; and, of course, the made-to-measure passes of Johnny Haynes. I also miss having to avoid getting trampled as George Cohen would power his way down the right wing, and I miss chuckling as his cross inevitably wound up in the raised arms of the fans behind the goal.

Yes, I miss the Cottage and the good times I had there. I have always kept in touch with news from the club, and Craven Cottage will be kept even nearer and dearer to me by the photographs in this book. Enjoy!

CONTENTS

Acknowledgements

Thanks are due to the many people who have helped in all sorts of ways during the production of this book, and in particular to the following: Jean Lawler, Charles Walker, Alex Ferguson, Ian Cranna, David Lloyd, Richard Jones, Andrew Haines, Heather Thomas, Tracey Hubbard, Sandra Coles, Nigel Standerline, Marina Ristic, Tony Goodgame and Jimmy Dunkley.

Picture credits

All photographs are by Ken Coton, except for the following:
Gary Pearce: 195, pages 205 to 212, pages 248 to 250, 282 (18, 23), 283 (8, 10, 18, 26, 31)
Hulton Deutsch Collection: 11R, 12C, 13T, 14B, 15C, 17T, 17C, 19, 214T, 214C, 214B, 215T, 215C, 215B, 219BL, 219BR, 220T, 282 (6)
Press Association: 12B, 14T, 216B, 217C, 217B, 218T, 219C, 220C, 221T
Solo Syndication: 216T, 216C, 217T, 220B, 221B
Topham: 13C, 13B, 15T, 15B, 16C, 16B, 17B
Pearce-Turner Collection: 11L, 14C, 16T, 21T, 22B, 23BR, 24T, 32C, 33T, 41B, 218C, 218B, 219T, 221C, 258BR, 282 (5, 13, 20, 22, 26, 33, 34), 283 (1, 6, 12, 19, 23, 27, 29, 33)
National Monuments Record: 285T, 287T
Monte Fresco: 203B
Ashwater Publishing: 12T
T.S.N. Canada: 5

INTRODUCTION

It had been a long-cherished dream of mine to produce a book of my Fulham photographs—but this is not exactly it! For that I have to thank the other co-producers of this book. Some months ago, as the football world was contemplating the dreadful prospect of Fulham leaving Craven Cottage, they had the splendid idea that perhaps the time had come to produce a book celebrating the club's more happy times. The club's 'golden years', they concluded, were from 1958 to 1983. These years coincided more or less with my times as the club's photographer, and so this book evolved, but bigger and better than I could ever have hoped. Happily, at the time of writing, Fulham are still at the Cottage. And it seems that the club's fortunes, so low in recent years, both on and off the field, may yet begin to revive. We all hope so, dear Fulham.

But it will take a lot to recapture the excitement, the drama, the glamour even, of the golden years covered by this book. The F.A. Cup run at the beginning of 1958 and the three Liverpool League Cup ties in November 1983 provide the natural starting and closing dates for this pictorial memoir; and in between came a Wembley appearance, another Cup semi-final, promotion three times, nine seasons in Division One—and a host of great players.

The book is not exactly a detailed history. One reason is that many historic moments remain unphotographed. I missed the match at Halifax in 1969, and didn't have my camera with me on Boxing Day in 1963. Also, I have put in the book the occasional picture that is not historically significant but which helps reflect the flavour of the times. And I have tried, also, to unearth from my negatives some pictures that have never been seen before.

The years prior to my time at the Cottage have been illustrated by photographs from agencies; the year or so after I left has been filled by Gary Pearce's splendid pictures, for which I am most grateful.

I was enormously privileged to be the club's photographer for most of these golden years. It was a magical time during which I saw many great players through my viewfinder. (Not even a Tuesday-night defeat at rain-soaked Darlington could ever take the edge off the pride I felt at being Fulham's picture chronicler!) I was always treated with kindness by staff and players at the club and I thank them all for making my time there so happy.

And so to a few more thanks. Without doubt, this book would never have appeared without the prompting and encouragement of my co-producers, all Fulham fanatics like me. So, many thanks to: Dennis Turner, debonair wordsmith and editorial whizz-kid; Fulham masterminds Dave Pearce and Alex White; the effervescent Yvonne Haines, organiser of the book's marketing and distribution; and Dave Gardner, who spared me any involvement with the financial side of the project. I learnt early on that all would go smoothly if I did exactly what I was told. I did and it did. It means that the result is truly a joint effort.

One note of apology. Most of the pictures feature forwards and goals, and it is a sorry fact that Fulham's goalkeepers and defenders don't get as much coverage. But, in my defence, I recall that fans always used to ask me after a match: 'Did you get the goals, Ken?'

On a personal note may I thank my father for his wisdom in taking me as a young lad to Fulham, and for his special encouragement during the time I've worked on this book. Also, thanks to Frank Flanagan, who, through his friendship with Johnny Haynes, secured my first photographer's passes, which led to me becoming the club's photographer.

Finally, a very special thank-you to the subscribers—including a number of former players—whose contributions enabled the book to be published. It was genuinely touching that so many were prepared to pay in advance for this venture. Those of us who have produced the book hope you like the final product—a book you all helped to create.

Ken Coton September 1992

SUBSCRIBERS

PRESENTATION COPIES
Graham Leggat   Johnny Haynes   Alec Stock
Ken Coton   Dave Gardner   Yvonne Haines   Dave Pearce   Dennis Turner   Alex White

1 Heather Thomas
2 Tracey Hubbard
3 Andrew Haines
4 Sandra Coles
5 Helen Drinkwater
6 Les Barrett
7 G J & S Davies
8 Andrew Homes
9 Jonathan Bureau
10 Mr Carlo Roberto BA
11 Nick Wood
12 Mr D M Booth
13 Charlie Wood
14 Philip Howard Bennett
15 Brian Clarke
16 Jean Lawler
17 Frances & Allan Gould
18 John C Friend
19 Raymond C Brooks
20 Dennis Bone
21 Eugene & Daniel Smyth
22 Michael Saunders
23 David Pearce
24 Ian Clarke
25 Robert A Fennell
26 Alfred G Fennell (in memoriam)
27 Mr David E Whisker
28 Ian McKay
29 Jeremy Helm
30 David King
31 John Delaney
32 Derek Ollis
33 David Evans
34 Allan J Youle
35 Dave Bell
36 Roger Scoon
37 Geoffrey Gordon Trieb
38 Ian Gray
39 John Stephens
40 Michael B Southcott
41 Barry Sklan
42 Keith Evemy
43 David Evemy
44 Dean Antony Gadd
45 James T McCrann
46 Joseph Aloysius Evinson
47 Malcolm Mears
48 Terence E Kebbell
49 Geoffrey P Kebbell
50 Mr N J U Urquhart
51 Allan Lunn
52 Norman William Reynolds
53 Jim Cox
54 Mr J L Jones
55 Mr D Bailey
56 John Shirley
57 Dave & Chris Clark
58 John MacDermott
59 Andrew S Victory
60 Alex Ferguson
61 Alan & Christopher Garner
62 Ray Brooks
63 J K Smith
64 John Page
65 Peter Fisher
66 Stephen Fisher
67 Chris Finn
68 John Aldridge
69 Jonathan Sim
70 Mr Peter Reason
71 Mr R J Gillett
72 Norman Swaffield
73 Michael John Brooks
74 J W Palmer
75 Jeff Palmer
76 Don Way
77 Roger Martin Puckey
78 Graham John Puckey
79 Frank Palmer
80 David Palmer
81 Peter Sharp
82 R M Wolny
83 Wayne Flitton
84 Alan Wicks
85 Gordon C M Thumwood
86 Philip Dear
87 Paul Dupille
88 Roy MacFarlane
89 Mr Alan J Gibbs
90 Tom Greatrex
91 Terry Kilroy
92 Harry Hawkins
93 Michael W Foot & Wendy A Foot
94 Barry McCann
95 Hugh McCann
96 Simon Foster
97 Dave Wharin
98 Mr D Izzard
99 Adrian Titcombe
100 John Mitchell
101 Andrew Jeffries
102 Graham Spackman
103 Steve Barry
104 David Daly
105 Jim Donnan
106 Graham Macdonald
107 John Barrett
108 Chris Watkins
109 Nicholas Orosz
110 James Clement
111 Neil Farrell
112 Thomas Gerard Farrell
113 Andrew R Wilson
114 Martin Plumb
115 Gerry Plumb
116 Jerry Lee
117 Martin Andrew Lee
118 Rob Bruce
119 E R Tonkin
120 Jim Picott
121 G R White
122 Peter Dearsley
123 Stuart Dearsley
124 David Gutteridge
125 Phil Petherick
126 Mr Patrick Barker
127 Peter Wale
128 D C Butler
129 Mr R E Booth
130 H W Scott
131 Cliff Moore
132 Nick Ivey
133 John Ivey
134 Ray Green
135 Dave & Mike Beasley
136 Martin Beasley
137 T J Turner
138 T J Turner
139 A Darke
140 Linda Gilbert
141 Colin A Carlin
142 Terence Beringham & Wendy Mitchell
143 Paul & Barry Taylor
144 Clare & Sue Taylor
145 David Tross
146 Martin & Catherine Goldthorpe
147 F E Creates
148 Colin & Joy Barnes
149 John Henry Hilton
150 Mr P M Grinham
151 Allan Blair
152 Louis Blair
153 Barbara Bowden
154 Derek J Ridgwell
155 Cyril E Pegram
156 Graham E Pegram
157 Doris Pegram
158 Matthew J Perry
159 Mrs Stella Crawford
160 Peter Bird
161 Reg Evans
162 Reg Evans
163 Andrew Steels
164 Steven Leven
165 David Page
166 Jim Sims
167 Alex Sims
168 Andy Sims
169 Ali Sims
170 Colin J Williams
171 John Ostinelli
172 R H Francis
173 R H Francis
174 R H Francis
175 Derek Van Ryne
176 Mr P J Jacobs
177 Richard Coward
178 Wendy & Dennis Ward
179 Mandy & Clive Ward
180 Derek George Patman
181 Ian F Woolley
182 Francis W Woolley
183 Bernard Showan
184 L H Brunwin
185 C L Brunwin
186 D A Brunwin
187 Geraldine Corkhill
188 Frederick J Wheeler
189 Mr W J Haynes
190 Richard, Chris & Neal Jones
191 Mark Callann
192 Steve & Tom Knight
193 D F Howard
194 John Alexander Taylor
195 Raymond M Rutt & Miss Barbara Rutt
196 E R Brunwin
197 P R Brunwin
198 J D Rowe
199 John Clinton
200 Nicholas Cloke
201 Jonathan Baines
202 James & Vincent Bottacchi
203 John Went
204 J Duggan
205 Matthew Turner
206 Tony Sparrow
207 Graham Weight
208 Steve Wears
209 Mr Keith John Dumas
210 Mr Keith John Dumas
211 Alan Charles Perryman
212 Mr & Mrs D R Hance
213 Jeremy Dearmer
214 Jason Johnson
215 Vaughan Daly
216 Kevin O'Callaghan
217 Patrick Mascall
218 Steve Carlsson
219 Geoff Carlsson
220 James Gardner
221 Gary Inwood
222 Michael Peter Durban
223 Edwin Arthur Wilder
224 Eddie Hales
225 Jane Blight
226 William S Hoadley
227 George Edward Hewitt
228 Peter T Yates
229 Colin R Cooper
230 Mr M F Sayers
231 Mr W E Cox
232 Dominic Lang
233 Clive Page
234 Alan Legge
235 Ian Cranna
236 Pam Dillon
237 Chris & Mick Best
238 Mr R Weller
239 Gerard Lyons
240 Annette Lyons
241 Emily Anne Lyons
242 Brian Hills
243 Simon Rowe
244 Christopher J Wheeler
245 Mr P T C Killen
246 John Farnham
247 Mr John Seal
248 Tony Walden
249 Frederick Robert Alford
250 Dr Dennis Brian Ring
251 Simon Cox
252 R G J M Earl & Carole King-Hele
253 D K Showan & W P Davies
254 Alan Shaw & Robert Shaw
255 Col G H T Shrimpton CBE TD
256 Ian Went
257 John F Yates
258 John F Yates
259 Roger Cross
260 D C N Malcolm
261 John C Galea
262 William O'Connell
263 Edward & Valerie Alexander
264 Stephen George Surridge
265 Gary Collier
266 Mr G Sheppard
267 Tony & Guy Sutlieff
268 Jerry Cope
269 Ian C Reid
270 Peter Donnison
271 Richard Wheeler
272 Phil Hannam
273 Diana Hort
274 Dave & Alison Salisbury
275 Derek Brewer
276 David William Dale
277 Tim McKay
278 Norman A Planes
279 Robin & Dennis Greaves
280 T W Wheeler
281 D J Wheeler
282 Mr C A Shailer
283 Mr F A Kenny
284 Michael Brame
285 Eric John Richards-Clark
286 John Wearmouth
287 Brian Longhurst
288 Lynn Hawes
289 Vivien Hildrey
290 Sally Johnston
291 John Martin
292 Barry Leaver
293 Tony Collins
294 Ken Simpson

295 Mrs S D Clark & Mr M Clark
296 William Moss (in memoriam)
297 Michael Wontner-Riches
298 Andrew Paul Vinken
299 Henry Stacey
300 Paul Langford
301 Iain Kilpatrick
302 David Winton
303 John Corner
304 Robert James French
305 Steve Moggridge
306 David M Hancock
307 Jim Nott
308 David Nott
309 Nigel F Reed
310 Stephen Jarvis
311 Colin Adaway
312 Hans Schut
313 James Driscoll
314 James Driscoll
315 Christopher Moggridge
316 Andrew Morris
317 Donald T Fribbins
318 Robin P Fribbins
319 Chas B Dean
320 Mike Ryley
321 Paul Hatcher
322 Tom Blomfield
323 John C Evans
324 Vic Reed
325 Paul Jackson
326 Jim & Steve Larking
327 Janice Smart
328 D J Tinson
329 David Lloyd
330 Benjamin James McCarthy
331 Ian Wilson
332 Allan Wilson
333 Paul Enticknap
334 Frank Enticknap
335 Spike Denton
336 John Morris
337 Edward Morris
338 Chris Mason
339 Dylan Mason
340 Ray Powell
341 Steven Battams
342 Eric Tinson
343 Mike Lownsbrough
344 Derek W Garner
345 Melvin Tenner
346 Melvin Tenner
347 Bob Howes
348 Bill Bateman
349 Keith Couling
350 Brian Wright
351 Mary Harris
352 B R T Blackman
353 G A P Blackman
354 Peter James Lenton
355 Craig Foley
356 Nina Robinson
357 Mrs Winifred Jones
358 Christopher Joseph Mandry
359 Alexandra Mandry
360 Stephen Richards
361 Sam Leigh
362 Charles Henry Ward (Ward Family)
363 John Fraser
364 Maureen & Brian Frith
365 Mrs M L Catt

366 Mrs M L Catt
367 Brian Pickering
368 Dominic Pickering
369 Austin Pickering
370 John Gillett
371 Mr B L Price
372 Steve P Child
373 Mr J Child
374 David Wilson
375 Neil Parmenter
376 Alfred Workman
377 Robert Joseph Taylor
378 Ken Owen
379 Steven Rayner
380 L S Bayliss
381 Peter Ward
382 David M Barnard
383 Kit Cooper
384 Daniel Taylor
385 Jon Busby
386 Leighton A Howe
387 John Whittock
388 Jeremy L Pruce
389 Edward Pink
390 Ian Spittles
391 Steve Owen
392 Mr D Young
393 Chris Copus
394 Barry S Myers
395 R A Read
396 R J Palmer
397 R D Palmer
398 John Garofall
399 Albert E Fox
400 Peter Phillips
401 Richard Shore
402 The Hills Family
403 Mr D J Martin
404 Stan Brown
405 Mrs C Julien
406 David Grossel
407 Mr R M Kelland
408 Chris & Sally Gerrard
409 Robert L Sopp
410 Philip Broadhurst
411 Wiard Meiis
412 K G Hutson
413 R & I Ambrose
414 Gerard Curran
415 Russell Joel Percy
416 David L Allen
417 Lionel C Allen
418 Colin Kempster
419 Paul Everett
420 T Handorff
421 A Knowles
422 Nick & Oli Woodward
423 Bill & Biddy Bates
424 Patrick John McNeela
425 Patrick Alfred McNeela
426 Roy Chute
427 R P Twynam
428 Barrie M Gale
429 Mrs S A Stevens
430 Mark A Stevens
431 Mark Everett
432 Simon Denton
433 Paul Dillon
434 Mrs Sarah L Haynes
435 Simon P Robbins
436 Philip R Hayes
437 Robert E Hayes
438 Mr & Mrs P D O'Connor
439 Mr & Mrs K P O'Connor
440 Ernst M Feibusch

441 Brian Newson
442 Bernard Donovan
443 Alan Cooper
444 Barry Cooper
445 Colin Newson
446 Thomas Murphy
447 Charles Corkery
448 Stephen Richard Quilty
449 John Cook
450 Rob Harding
451 Mr R F Roper
452 Kenneth David Henderson
453 Andrew Cole
454 Robert Heath
455 Frankie Power
456 Dave Ellender
457 Tom & Heather Young
458 Carol J Woodman
459 D M Davies
460 P McQueen
461 Edward Lowe
462 M McPherson
463 Gary & Carol See
464 Mr J B Duffy
465 Stuart John Dymond
466 Paul James Rust
467 John & Michael Rust
468 Colin Stevens
469 Rosemarie Conroy
470 Alan Stevens
471 Theo Morris
472 Kim Matthews
473 M E Le Jeune
474 Sean Deasy
475 Les Way
476 Terry, Glyn & Lee Williams
477 Ronald Thomas
478 Stephen P Magee
479 John Harrison
480 C J Brereton
481 John V Hill
482 Mr Peter Ray
483 David Johnson
484 Nada Savitch
485 John Dennett
486 Kevin Lovett
487 Graham Ogston
488 Mr C W Cox
489 Mr F J Herman
490 David Christopher Baines
491 Stuart Hoskin
492 Jez Bryant
493 John R Friend
494 Ian McCulloch
495 Bob Sulatycki
496 Tim Rowley
497 Michael Hopgood
498 Nicola Blake
499 Alison Marks
500 P I Cooper
501 Kenneth Lock
502 C J W Bailey
503 F W Bailey
504 Mr L J Kirkham
505 Mr M A Maunders
506 Jane Knivett
507 Ron Greenstreet
508 Mr David Charles Norman
509 Mr Joseph Ridge
510 Mr Lance Phillips
511 Mr John Phillips
512 Ted Darling
513 Julian M Church

514 Mr Joseph Palmer
515 Mrs Betty Palmer
516 Morgan D Phillips
517 Robert M Page
518 Mr & Mrs D Breden
519 Paul Hooper
520 Gerry Peyton
521 Mrs J Rivers
522 Mr John Murray
523 Richard Dazeley
524 Martyn Lundie
525 Mrs V J K Myers
526 Ray Brooks
527 Len & Martin Timms
528 John Neil
529 Michael Pearson
530 C N Pullen
531 Christopher S Payne
532 Miss C Chambers
533 Bruce Dunn
534 John Spreadbury
535 Dominic Guard
536 Bodo Wedemeier
537 Mick Burgess
538 Alan Warner
539 John Alexsander White
540 John Alexsander White
541 Brian C Sibley
542 John Morris
543 Mr J D Sullivan
544 John Dempsey
545 Mark James Waghorn
546 Adrian Cotton
547 Malcolm A Scott
548 J R Probert
549 Nick Spokes
550 Mr Ian Ward
551 Ian C A Parkin
552 Michael & Elizabeth Lawrence
553 R Jones
554 Neil Smith
555 Anthony Smith
556 Ian Gardner
557 Neil Gardner
558 Valerie M English
559 Sidney Chase
560 Alfred Bath
561 Cyril A Swain
562 Vanessa & Alan Fisher
563 David M Chelley
564 Alan Hopping
565 Bob Lipscombe
566 Graham Lipscombe
567 Mr Edward Hagreen (Monty)
568 Mr A K Honeybone
569 Stephen Roy Hills
570 Mr Graham Monk
571 P R Bingham
572 Jeremy Alexander
573 Rod Alexander
574 Michael Caddy
575 David A Emery
576 Mr Nigel Davey
577 Gary Smith
578 Raymond & Alan Rudd
579 Mrs Joan Baxter
580 Roger Sells
581 Olive Hayes
582 Peter Smith
583 Ray Disson
584 Michael Roots
585 Desmond Fox
586 Chris Harte
587 Barrie J Railton

588 Alec Keith
589 Mark Lawson
590 Tom Sperlinger
591 Peter Thomson
592 Peter Heffernan
593 Mrs M A Doughty
594 Stephen Alan Slade
595 John Gregory
596 Ian Gregory
597 Steve Murrell
598 Mr Bill Jenkins
599 David Francis
600 Peter C Bonner
601 Nick Jenkins
602 C J Hegarty
603 Tosh Chamberlain
604 Fred Callaghan
605 Anthony Ramos
606 Helge Eriksen
607 Steve Peterkin
608 Christopher Hilton
609 David N Millard
610 Barry Adams
611 F G Hunt
612 Sally Turberville
613 Sally Turberville
614 Abelardo Martinez
615 Patrick Keefe
616 Keith Horstead
617 Alan Squire
618 David Sweiry
619 Roger Lowman
620 Graham & Rosemary Dolphin
621 Dave Wellington
622 Stephen Walton
623 Andy Walton
624 Mike Taylor
625 Derek Hicks
626 Desmond M Lynch
627 John Walters
628 Paul Martinez
629 Noel Preston
630 Graham & Sandy Preston
631 Bobby Keetch
632 David Roodyn
633 Derry Quigley
634 Antony Tune
635 Mel Morris
636 Sarah Morris
637 S P O'Keeffe
638 G I S Hortop
639 John Gordon
640 Roger Wettone
641 Alan Smith
642 Robert Turner
643 Jimmy Dunkley
644 Mike Mildren
645 Sigrid Stevenson
646 Tony Gale
647 Jim Langley
648 Alan Mullery
649 David Hamilton
650 Mr J C Cross
651 Jimmy Hill
652 Geoff Buckwell
653 Gary Piper

Seasons 1958-59 to 1961-62

During 1958, Fulham's fortunes took an upward turn. In March, the club reached the semi-finals of the F.A. Cup, losing only after a replay. By the end of the season, a few weeks later, they had narrowly missed promotion to Division One, but, after the summer break, they began the campaign that did finally lead to promotion.

Throughout that 1958-59 season, the club remained in one of the top two positions, eventually finishing as runners-up. The following season they finished in the top half of Division One for the only time in their history. After a promising start in 1960-61, they fell away in the last three months but were still comfortably clear of the relegation zone. These three seasons were the most successful phase in the club's history.

In the summer of 1958 there were some important changes at the club. Bedford Jezzard, Fulham's record scorer, replaced the departed Dug Livingstone in the manager's office, working in tandem with secretary and general manager Frank Osborne. At the turn of the year, director Tommy Trinder took over the chairmanship following the death of Charles Dean. On the field, Jezzard's first incursion into the transfer market led to the acquisition of Graham Leggat from Aberdeen, one of Fulham's best post-war signings. He succeeded Roy Dwight, who had moved on to Nottingham Forest. In the final promotion push, Alan Mullery was drafted into the side, and with Tony Macedo in goal and George Cohen at right back, the Cottagers could boast three of the most promising young defenders in the country.

By the spring of 1961, a number of loyal club figures were reaching the end of their careers. Robin Lawler, Roy Bentley and Jimmy Hill, who between them had made over 750 appearances for Fulham and were regulars in the 1958-59 promotion team, made way for younger players like Johnny Key and Brian O'Connell. Throughout this period, the Cottage faithful were privileged to see the Maestro, Johnny Haynes, at the height of his powers. Haynes, appointed England captain in 1960, was ably supported by stalwarts like Jim Langley, Eddie Lowe, Maurice Cook and Tosh Chamberlain, and together, the new and old, the young and not-so-young, combined to produce as good a side as Fulham have had in their 113-year existence.

Before Ken Coton took up the post in about 1962, the club had no official photographer. Readers of the programme of this era will recall the same poorly reproduced portrait shots appearing with monotonous regularity. The pictures in this section have been obtained from photographic agencies, and are a representative rather than a comprehensive sample of the period. There is enough evidence here, however, to give a real flavour of the time when crowds regularly topped 30,000, when the action took place in the penalty areas rather than the centre circle, and when the players and the fans seemed to share the enjoyment of the occasion.

The 1958-59 season opened in the manner it was to continue—with a convincing home victory. Stoke were crushed 6-1, and Graham Leggat, Fulham's summer signing from Aberdeen, scored the first of his 134 goals for the club (right). Coincidentally, his 134th goal, eight years later, was also against Stoke.

An important change behind the scenes during that summer of 1958 was the appointment of Bedford Jezzard as team manager, in succession to Dugald Livingstone.

Away travel, 1958 style. Smart blazers, club ties and white shirts. In the coach are Tony Barton, Ken Collins (half hidden behind Barton), Alan Mullery, with Roy Bentley and Johnny Haynes peering out. Standing outside are Arthur Stevens, Trevor Chamberlain, Maurice Cook, Jimmy Hill, Jim Langley, Robin Lawler, Eddie Lowe, George Cohen, Frank Penn (trainer), and Beddy Jezzard (manager).

The cornerstone of Fulham's defence for several seasons was the trio of goalkeeper Tony Macedo, and full-backs George Cohen and Jim Langley, all of whom were to win England recognition. Here they line up to thwart a Lincoln attack.

During the promotion campaign, Johnny Haynes emerged as a prolific goalscorer. In the match against Lincoln, he scored all four in the 4-2 victory. His first goal is shown below. Haynes scored three more hat-tricks that season.

During 1958-59, Fulham established a club record of 18 League home victories in a season. Sheffield United were beaten 4-2 in November, and the scoring was opened when England international goalkeeper Alan Hodgkinson fumbled a speculative Johnny Key effort (right). The match was full of action at both ends, and in the picture below, Macedo clears a determined challenge from Russell, suported by Roy Bentley, George Cohen and Robin Lawler. Players of both sides are wearing black armbands in memory of Harry Bamford, a long-serving Bristol Rovers full-back who had been killed in a road accident.

Rovers provided the opponents at the Cottage at the end of January 1959. The bottom picture shows Leggat challenging goalkeeper Norman, while Maurice Cook looks on. It was Cook's goal that settled the match.

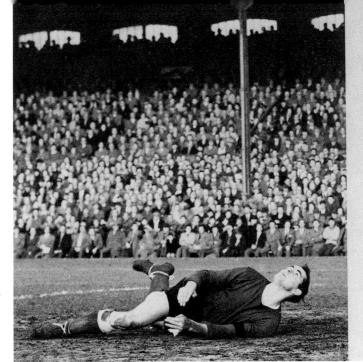

		P	W	D	L	F	A	Pts
1	Sheff Wed	42	28	6	8	106	48	62
2	**Fulham**	**42**	**27**	**6**	**9**	**96**	**61**	**60**
3	Sheff United	42	23	7	12	82	48	53
4	Liverpool	42	24	5	13	87	62	53
5	Stoke	42	21	7	14	72	58	49
6	Bristol Rovers	42	18	12	12	80	64	48
7	Derby	42	20	8	14	74	71	48
8	Charlton	42	18	7	17	92	90	43
9	Cardiff	42	18	7	17	65	65	43
10	Bristol City	42	17	7	18	74	70	41
11	Swansea	42	16	9	17	79	81	41
12	Brighton	42	15	11	16	74	90	41
13	Middlesbrough	42	15	10	17	87	71	40
14	Huddersfield	42	16	8	18	62	55	40
15	Sunderland	42	16	8	18	64	75	40
16	Ipswich	42	17	6	19	62	77	40
17	Leyton Orient	42	14	8	20	71	78	36
18	Scunthorpe	42	12	9	21	55	84	33
19	Lincoln	42	11	7	24	63	93	29
20	Rotherham	42	10	9	23	42	82	29
21	Grimsby	42	9	10	23	62	90	28
22	Barnsley	42	10	7	25	55	91	27

DIVISION TWO 1958-59 Final League Table

Fulham's first season back in the top flight—1959-60—proved to be their best ever at this level. Home form was particularly impressive. Haynes celebrated his 25th birthday by helping Fulham to a 4-3 victory over Newcastle at the Cottage. The top picture shows what proved to be the winning goal, scored by Jimmy Hill (obscured by the goal-post), whilst Newcastle players stand by helplessly.

Above: The First Division first-team squad. Back row: George Cohen, Ken Collins, Joe Stapleton, Derek Lampe, Eddie Lowe, Tony Barton, Tony Macedo, Alan Mullery; front: John Doherty, Jimmy Hill, Roy Bentley, Tosh Chamberlain, Mike Johnson, Graham Leggat, Robin Lawler, Johnny Haynes.

By the end of November, Fulham were challenging for the leadership of Division One. Their position was strengthened by a 1-0 win over Burnley, the eventual champions. The goal that won the match (left) was a bizarre looping header from Jimmy Hill.

As Graham Leggat mentions in his foreword to this book, the backroom staff at the Cottage made a significant contribution to the happy atmosphere. Here coach Arthur Stevens, watched by groundsman Albert Purdy, assistant trainer Joe Bacuzzi, and long-serving trainer Frank Penn, inspects the frozen pitch before the match against Everton in January 1960. Notwithstanding the snow, the match took place, and Fulham won 2-0.

Below: Despite being 'protected' by Langley, Lawler, Cohen, Lowe and Cook, Macedo is beaten by Birmingham's Stubbs. The match ended 2-2.

A highlight of the season was the defeat of Arsenal 0-3 at the Cottage on Easter Monday. The opening goal, shown at the bottom of the page, was scored by Johnny Key past a despairing Kelsey, but Key is not in the picture.

DIVISION ONE 1959-60 Final League Table

		P	W	D	L	F	A	Pts
1	Burnley	42	24	7	11	85	61	55
2	Wolves	42	24	6	12	106	67	54
3	Tottenham	42	21	11	10	86	50	53
4	West Brom	42	19	11	12	83	57	49
5	Sheff Wed	42	19	11	12	80	59	49
6	Bolton	42	20	8	14	59	51	48
7	Man United	42	19	7	16	102	80	45
8	Newcastle	42	18	8	16	82	78	44
9	Preston	42	16	12	14	79	76	44
10	**Fulham**	**42**	**17**	**10**	**15**	**73**	**80**	**44**
11	Blackpool	42	15	10	17	59	71	40
12	Leicester	42	13	13	16	66	75	39
13	Arsenal	42	15	9	18	68	80	39
14	West Ham	42	16	6	20	75	91	38
15	Man City	42	17	3	22	78	84	37
16	Everton	42	13	11	18	73	78	37
17	Blackburn	42	16	5	21	60	70	37
18	Chelsea	42	14	9	19	76	91	37
19	Birmingham	42	13	10	19	63	80	36
20	Nottm Forest	42	13	9	20	50	74	35
21	Leeds	42	12	10	20	65	92	34
22	Luton	42	9	12	21	50	73	30

F^FC
1960-61
DIVISION ONE

The goals continued to flow in 1960-61,
although results were more erratic. In
the first match, against Cardiff, Graham
Leggat opened Fulham's account for the
season with an unstoppable drive past
goalkeeper Vearncombe (top).

A fortnight later, Birmingham were
beaten at the Cottage 2-1. Here Maurice
Cook is denied by the cross-bar, but he
later scored the winning goal.

There was a moment to savour in the
middle of September, when Chelsea
were defeated 3-2 at the Cottage.
Fulham's winning goal was scored by
Johnny Haynes, despite the attentions
of Bobby Evans, Peter Bonetti and John
Sillett. In the background can be seen a
young Terry Venables.

16

Fulham recorded their fifth consecutive home win at the end of September when they defeated Preston 2-0. Maurice Cook (above) and Jim Langley, from the penalty spot, were the scorers.

The going got heavier as autumn turned to winter, but an exciting 4-3 victory over Blackpool at the end of February put the Cottagers on a winning trail. Had Macedo not denied Charnley (below), a point may well have been dropped.

17

This was one of the first pictures that photographer Ken Coton ever took at the Cottage; it was during the match against Leicester on 12th November 1960. The photograph captures well the atmosphere of big-time matches of the era. Unfortunately, Ken cannot recall whether the incident shown—a shot by Johnny Key—actually was the goal that Key scored that day. If it was, no doubt a hat or two would have been raised in celebration.

DIVISION ONE 1960-61 Final League Table

		P	W	D	L	F	A	Pts
1	Tottenham	42	31	4	7	115	55	66
2	Sheff Wed	42	23	12	7	78	47	58
3	Wolves	42	25	7	10	103	75	57
4	Burnley	42	22	7	13	102	77	51
5	Everton	42	22	6	14	87	69	50
6	Leicester	42	18	9	15	87	70	45
7	Man United	42	18	9	15	88	76	45
8	Blackburn	42	15	13	14	77	76	43
9	Aston Villa	42	17	9	16	78	77	43
10	West Brom	42	18	5	19	67	71	41
11	Arsenal	42	15	11	16	77	85	41
12	Chelsea	42	15	7	20	98	100	37
13	Man City	42	13	11	18	79	90	37
14	Nottm Forest	42	14	9	19	62	78	37
15	Cardiff	42	13	11	18	60	85	37
16	West Ham	42	13	10	19	77	88	36
17	**Fulham**	**42**	**14**	**8**	**20**	**72**	**95**	**36**
18	Bolton	42	12	11	19	58	73	35
19	Birmingham	42	14	6	22	62	84	34
20	Blackpool	42	12	9	21	68	73	33
21	Newcastle	42	11	10	21	86	109	32
22	Preston	42	10	10	22	43	71	30

SEASON 1961-62

DIVISION ONE

The season got off to a less than encouraging start, with three of the first four games ending in defeats. One of these reverses came in a home game against Manchester City. Fulham were leading 3-0 at the interval, but City staged a dramatic second half recovery to win 4-3, the winner coming in the last minute.

Form quickly improved, however. From the start of September, just one of the next 11 League matches was lost, and by the end of October, a creditable position of fifth had been reached. Victories

Back row: George Cohen, Alan Mullery, Tony Macedo, Jimmy Langley, Eddie Lowe, Derek Lampe; front: Johnny Key, Brian O'Connell, Johnny Haynes, John Doherty, Trevor Watson.

came in successive away games at Bolton and at Portman Road, where Alf Ramsey was steering Ipswich to the Championship in their very first season in the top flight.

The next four months were disastrous. Of the 15 games played, 14 were lost, including a record-breaking seven successive home defeats. Bottom club Chelsea came to the Cottage for the first game of the New Year, and won 4-3. Making his debut for Fulham that day was Jackie Henderson, newly signed from Arsenal for

£14,000, but he was unable to inspire the team to a much needed win. In sharp contrast was the form in the F.A. Cup, where progress to the semi-final was relatively unimpeded.

With title-chasing Burnley waiting in the semi-final, mid-March found the Cottagers four points adrift at the bottom. The long overdue win finally came at home to high-flying Sheffield United, when a Maurice Cook hat-trick inspired a 5-2 victory, the turning point of the League campaign. This was quickly followed by a morale-boosting 3-0 win away to fellow strugglers Cardiff City. Although the Cup semi-final was disappointingly lost, the League revival stayed on course. Wins over Arsenal, Blackburn, Wolves and a draw against Spurs, put Fulham two points clear of bottom clubs Cardiff and Chelsea.

Defeats in the two Easter matches against West Brom put the Cottagers back in trouble. Cardiff and Fulham were level on points with two matches remaining, though Fulham had the better goal average. While Cardiff were losing at Everton, goals from Leggat and Cook secured the points at home to Manchester United for what was to be the first of the 'great escapes'.

F F C
1961-62
DIVISION ONE

Fulham threw away a 3-0 lead in their first home match of the 1961-62 season against Manchester City, and lost 3-4. This Langley penalty goal was an early attempt at close-up action by photographer Ken Coton, and the picture failed to show the ball... However, he made no mistake three days later with the picture, below, of Maurice Cook's goal against Everton.

The other goal in the 2-1 victory that day against Everton (top opposite) came from John Doherty (not in the picture). The photo below it shows a view rarely seen today—an old-fashioned one-to-one as Langley faces Everton's Roy Parnell with almost half of the pitch to themselves.

FFC
1961-62
DIVISION ONE

It became a habit for Fulham to take two points from Leicester in the 1960s, and that is just what happened when the teams met in September 1961. Tosh Chamberlain was on the mark for Fulham (top opposite), as was Graham Leggat, although his shot (shown at centre opposite) narrowly missed the target. Aston Villa were well beaten, 3-1, at the Cottage in October, but this time (left) goalkeeper Nigel Sims and full-back John Neal stopped Brian O'Connell.

West Ham went down 2-0 a fortnight later, and the opening goal (top) was scored by Alan Mullery. No. 6 for the Hammers was Bobby Moore who, 14 years later, would play a big part in one of Fulham's finest moments, alongside 'Mullers'. Above: Johnny Haynes sends over another tantalising cross for Leggat to score Fulham's second goal against the Hammers. Right: Fulham's catastrophic slide started in November with a 1-0 defeat at home to Blackpool—part of a run of 14 defeats in 15 games (including seven home defeats on the trot). If Doherty, Leggat or O'Connell had done more with this cross, perhaps the final third of the season might have been less nerve-racking.

Despite the poor run of results, there was no sense of panic. In defence, Bill Dodgin and Eddie Lowe (shown left in the defeat by Blackpool), together with George Cohen, missed only eight appearances between them throughout the whole season. Cohen is pictured in the match with Nottingham Forest, which ended 1-1 and stopped the losing sequence.

MATCH OF THE SEASON
Fulham 5 Sheffield United 2
17th March 1962

This match was to prove a turning-point in Fulham's First Division life. Despite progressing to the semi-finals of the F.A. Cup, a run of 11 defeats and one draw had left them at the foot of the table, six points adrift of safety. A win in this midweek fixture was vital.

Without three of their best players (Hodgkinson, Shaw and Summers), the United defence was as open as Ilkley Moor, and Maurice Cook revelled in the freedom he was allowed. He opened the scoring with a splendid header after 15 minutes (top picture), and then helped set up goals for Graham Leggat and Eddie Lowe before the interval. After the break, Cookie completed his hat-trick (pictures above and below) to the delight of the 22,711 crowd. For the Blades, debutant Reg Matthewson, later a Fulham player, reduced the arrears, and with virtually the last kick of the game, Keith Kettleborough added their second to make the scoreline more respectable.

After this, Fulham's League form recovered. By winning five and drawing one of their last 10 games, they clawed their way to safety, and left Cardiff and Chelsea to face the drop.

John Doherty was a talented player who never fulfilled his potential. He ended his Fulham career against Forest in March. He made 57 League and Cup appearances between 1956 and March 1962. In this last match, he proved he was the equal of his marker (and the tree and the half-time scoreboard...) in the air.

DIVISION ONE 1961-62 Final League Table

		P	W	D	L	F	A	Pts
1	Ipswich	42	24	8	10	93	67	56
2	Burnley	42	21	11	10	101	67	53
3	Tottenham	42	21	10	11	88	69	52
4	Everton	42	20	11	11	88	54	51
5	Sheff United	42	19	9	14	61	69	47
6	Sheff Wed	42	20	6	16	72	58	46
7	Aston Villa	42	18	8	16	65	56	44
8	West Ham	42	17	10	15	76	82	44
9	West Brom	42	15	13	14	83	67	43
10	Arsenal	42	16	11	15	71	72	43
11	Bolton	42	16	10	16	62	66	42
12	Man City	42	17	7	18	78	81	41
13	Blackpool	42	15	11	16	70	75	41
14	Leicester	42	17	6	19	72	71	40
15	Man United	42	15	9	18	72	75	39
16	Blackburn	42	14	11	17	50	58	39
17	Birmingham	42	14	10	18	65	81	38
18	Wolves	42	13	10	19	73	86	36
19	Nottm Forest	42	13	10	19	63	79	36
20	**Fulham**	**42**	**13**	**7**	**22**	**66**	**74**	**33**
21	Cardiff	42	9	14	19	50	81	32
22	Chelsea	42	9	10	23	63	94	28

SEASON 1962-63

DIVISION ONE

After six years at West Bromwich Albion, Bobby Robson returned to the Cottage to link up again with England team-mate Johnny Haynes. The reunion didn't last long. With just two games of the season played, Haynes was involved in a serious car crash. The injury brought an abrupt end to his international career just two months after he had skippered England in the World Cup finals in Chile, and put his whole football future into doubt.

Leicester City were beaten 2-1 at home on the opening day, but, that apart, the first half of the campaign brought little joy. Just five wins before Christmas left the Cottagers one place and two

points above bottom club Leyton Orient. In a season effectively cut in half by one of the worst winters on record, the enforced winter break, which lasted six to seven weeks, gave the team respite from what was to become an all too regular fight against relegation.

When League football finally resumed, a complete turn-around occurred in the club's fortunes. A nine-match unbeaten run started with an away point at fellow strugglers Leyton Orient. The following Saturday brought a 3-1 victory at home to Nottingham Forest, the start of an eight-match winning run. Success came as readily away from home as it did at the Cottage. Notably, in the space of a few days, Fulham came away

Back row: Jim Langley, George Cohen, Alan Mullery, Tony Macedo, Eddie Lowe, Bobby Robson; front: Johnny Key, Graham Leggat, Maurice Cook, Stan Brown, Brian O'Connell.

from both Manchester United and Manchester City with maximum points. Fifteen goals and six clean sheets in the winning run took the club to mid-table and safety.

The season ended on a sentimental note with the end of Eddie Lowe's 13-year association with the club. In his final game, against Birmingham City at the Cottage, the visitors obligingly scored five of the six goals in a 3-3 draw.

On the opening day of the season, Fulham played hosts to Leicester, and Gordon Banks found that not even his outstanding skills could stop Graham Leggat. The Scottish international scored both goals (pictures left and right) in the Cottagers' 2-1 win.

MATCH OF THE SEASON

Fulham 1 Everton 0
1st September 1962

By the start of the 1962-63 season, Fulham supporters had become used to the idea of First Division football at the Cottage. This was the start of the fourth season in the top flight, exceeding the previous spell a decade earlier. After a brush with relegation the previous year, the club had made an uncertain start to the new campaign, one win and a draw in their first four games. To compound the problems, skipper Johnny Haynes was ruled out until the New Year after a serious car accident, and the recently returned Bobby Robson was missing with an ankle injury.

The 30,592 fans who packed into the Cottage that late summer afternoon to see this match must have feared the worst. Visitors Everton, inspired by Alex 'Golden Vision' Young, had made a 100% winning start to the season. Their four victories included a double over Manchester United, and the Toffees had scored 11 goals. On the day, however, the fight and enthusiasm of Fulham's young side rocked the League leaders. Makeshift centre-forward Stan Brown, in his third first-team outing, was the hero of the Cottage, with the only goal of the game in the first half.

Young Stan was to become a fixture in the side over the next decade and had another 394 games ahead of him. Everton were to bounce back from this reverse and were to finish season as champions. They clinched the title at Goodison in May with a 4-1 victory—over Fulham.

In his last season at Fulham, Eddie Lowe was still a tower of strength in defence; here, left, he is on hand to block Dennis Stevens.

Above: Bill Dodgin and Tony Macedo keep out the great Alex Young.

Right: The League leaders found the makeshift Fulham attack a handful, particularly the Cottagers' inside-right, Maurice Cook.

F^FC

1962-63
DIVISION ONE

The Cottage floodlights were switched on for the first time for the visit of Sheffield Wednesday in September. Fulham won 4-1. Maurice Cook got a hat-trick, and, but for Ron Springett, would have had a fourth (above). For the first half of the season, Scottish international Jackie Henderson was at inside-forward, but he got little joy when faced with his former Arsenal team-mates, who won 3-1. A Jimmy Langley goal that was not a penalty was a rarity, but he managed one at Nottingham Forest in October (below), though Fulham lost 3-1.

Opposite page: League champions Ipswich travelled to the Cottage in October and played out an entertaining 1-1 draw. Baxter found a way past Langley, Macedo and Cohen to score for the visitors, but Stan Brown, just establishing himself in the side, managed to score for Fulham. Apart from Baxter's effort, Macedo dealt competently with everything that Ipswich had to offer.

The two Manchester clubs were at the Cottage within a month of each other towards the end of the year, and both won. City beat Fulham 4-2 in what was the last of Derek Lampe's 96 games for the Cottagers (top). United would have won by more than 1-0 had Quixall not missed a penalty (above) on a frozen Boxing Day afternoon. The Big Freeze was about to begin, and Fulham's next League match at Craven Cottage was almost two months later. Nottingham Forest were the visitors, and Fulham's 3-1 win was sealed by Calvin Palmer's own goal.

1962-63
DIVISION ONE

Fulham's only First Division meeting with Leyton Orient at Brisbane Road was the very first match after the Big Freeze, on February 16th. The match marked Johnny Haynes' comeback after his road accident, and was drawn 1-1, though Stan Brown, still a centre-forward came close to winning it (above).

Goalkeeper Macedo was one of only two ever-presents in 1962-63, and a typically brave save at the feet of Blackburn's Bryan Douglas helped to earn a point in a goalless draw.

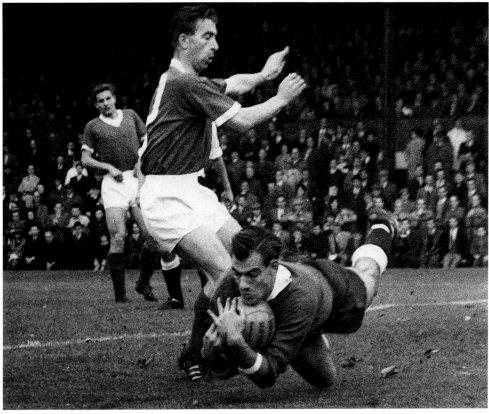

Fulham recorded a run of eight consecutive victories between the end of February and the beginning of April. Maurice Cook got the second goal in the 2-0 home win over Blackpool (above), and Graham Leggat scored the only goal of the game at Ipswich (left). The most spectacular goal came from debutant Rodney Marsh against Aston Villa in March. His stunning volley (below) gave goalkeeper John Gavan, another debutant, no chance, and Fulham won 1-0.

Right: Rodney Marsh, not visible in the picture of his Villa goal which appears on the opposite page, is, by recompense, shown in action here in the same match.

The last victory in Fulham's eight-match winning sequence was at home to West Ham. Johnny Key scored the second goal with a close-range effort (below), in the 2-0 win.

Burnley, as always, were difficult opponents. They ended the winning sequence at Turf Moor on Good Friday, but in the return on Easter Monday, owed much to the efforts of goalkeeper Adam Blacklaw (bottom picture) for taking a point in a 1-1 draw.

The goal against Burnley in the 1-1 home draw was scored by winger Johnny Key, who had stolen unmarked into the six-yard box; he gave Blacklaw no chance with this header.

DIVISION ONE 1962-63 Final League Table

		P	W	D	L	F	A	Pts
1	Everton	42	25	11	6	84	42	61
2	Tottenham	42	23	9	10	111	62	55
3	Burnley	42	22	10	10	78	57	54
4	Leicester	42	20	12	10	79	53	52
5	Wolves	42	20	10	12	93	65	50
6	Sheff Wed	42	19	10	13	77	63	48
7	Arsenal	42	18	10	14	86	77	46
8	Liverpool	42	17	10	15	71	59	44
9	Nottm Forest	42	17	10	15	67	69	44
10	Sheff United	42	16	12	14	58	60	44
11	Blackburn	42	15	12	15	79	71	42
12	West Ham	42	14	12	16	73	69	40
13	Blackpool	42	13	14	15	58	64	40
14	West Brom	42	16	7	19	71	79	39
15	Aston Villa	42	15	8	19	62	68	38
16	**Fulham**	**42**	**14**	**10**	**18**	**50**	**71**	**38**
17	Ipswich	42	12	11	19	59	78	35
18	Bolton	42	15	5	22	55	75	35
19	Man United	42	12	10	20	67	81	34
20	Birmingham	42	10	13	19	63	90	33
21	Man City	42	10	11	21	58	102	31
22	Leyton Orient	42	6	9	27	37	81	21

SEASON 1963-64

DIVISION ONE

After the previous two years of fighting for survival in the First Division, Fulham remained for the greater part of this season in a much healthier position. This owed much to an excellent home record, and only two games were lost at the Cottage. This was in stark contrast to the away form, which brought just two wins—at Chelsea and Leicester—in 21 trips. The Chelsea victory, with goals from Earle and O'Connell, was the club's first-ever success at Stamford Bridge. The

Back row: Bobby Robson, Bobby Keetch, Alan Mullery, Tony Macedo, George Cohen, Jim Langley; front: Johnny Key, Graham Leggat, Stan Brown, Maurice Cook, Johnny Haynes, Brian O'Connell.

Leicester victory came at a price, for 19-year-old Rodney Marsh, in scoring the winner, collided with a post, seriously injuring himself.

Injuries had also forced the use of three keepers in the first seven games. Dave Underwood, bought as cover in the close season from Watford, played most of the earlier games after Tony Macedo was injured against champions Everton on the opening day of the season. Third choice Martin Townsend had a less successful time, conceding eight goals in just two games.

From mid-November, with Macedo back in goal and Johnny Haynes playing as well as ever, the League position was consolidated with home wins against Wolves, Sheffield United and a record-breaking 10-1 victory against Ipswich on Boxing Day. In the return two days later, Ipswich exacted their revenge, though by a mere two-goal margin, winning 4-2.

By the end of January, Fulham reached their highest position of the season, 14th. Goals from Bobby Howfield and Johnny Haynes earned a 2-2 draw at Arsenal, the club's first-ever point at Highbury. In March, three teams chasing the League title came to the Cottage. Two of the games, against Manchester United and Spurs, ended all square. Eventual champions Liverpool were beaten by the only goal, scored by Reg Stratton, in what proved to be Alan Mullery's last game before his controversial move to Spurs, a decision that, in retrospect, contributed to Fulham's gradual decline.

The Cottagers took a bit of a battering in the opening games of the season, losing five of the first seven. A 1-4 defeat at Burnley in September was followed by a similar thrashing at home by Arsenal. In the picture above left, there are seven Arsenal players in attendance as Mullery goes up for a header in the visitors' penalty area. Bursts from Johnny Key (left) and Johnny Haynes (seen, above, beating Laurie Brown) made little impression on the Gunners' defence. Rather happier was the home match with Bolton later that month. Jim Langley's typically clinical penalty made the game safe for Fulham at 3-1.

1963-64
DIVISION ONE

Here are two more goals from the Bolton match, scored by Maurice Cook and Johnny Haynes.

F
F C
1963-64
DIVISION ONE

Opposite page: 'Going to the Match', 1963 style—and prices. The other picture shows one of the less appealing aspects of a visit to the Cottage for an opponent—the prospect of being tackled by Bobby Keetch, as Roy Vernon of Everton found out. The irrepressible Keetch, who was to footballing subtlety what Dylan Thomas was to sobriety, also found time in this match to go forward and score in the 2-2 draw, his first-ever goal in top-class football.

MATCH OF THE SEASON
Fulham 2 Manchester United 2
27th March 1964

Anyone who doubts that the 1960s really were the 'good old days' need only look at Fulham's fixture list for March 1964 which included, in an eight-day spell, home games against Liverpool, Manchester United and Spurs. None of these teams left the Cottage with maximum points.

The pick of the games was the Good Friday clash with Manchester United, and 41,769 packed into the ground to see it. Part of the attraction may well have been the first visit to the Cottage of United's new teenage sensation, George Best, who in only a handful of games had struck up a remarkable partnership with Law and Charlton. Fulham, still buzzing after a 1-0 victory over Liverpool, had young Fred Callaghan in for the recently transferred Alan Mullery. In Steve Earle, the Cottagers had their own exciting find, and it was he who levelled the scores in the second half (below), after Herd and Law had given United a 2-1 interval lead. Haynes was Fulham's other marksman (top).

This was a thoroughly entertaining encounter, with the honours deservedly shared. United missed out on the title this season, but were to win it the following year, and both Earle and Best were to feature in Fulham's history in subsequent seasons.

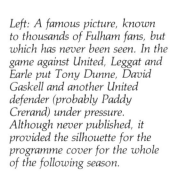

Left: A famous picture, known to thousands of Fulham fans, but which has never been seen. In the game against United, Leggat and Earle put Tony Dunne, David Gaskell and another United defender (probably Paddy Crerand) under pressure. Although never published, it provided the silhouette for the programme cover for the whole of the following season.

A visit from Spurs was always a highlight in the Cottage calendar, and the match in April 1964 provided fine entertainment. In the top picture, Bobby Robson fires in a shot before former team-mate Alan Mullery can put in a tackle. Fulham's goal in the 1-1 draw came from Haynes (hidden amongst defenders, above). He eluded Mullery to fire the ball past Bill Brown.

	DIVISION ONE 1963-64 Final League Table							
		P	**W**	**D**	**L**	**F**	**A**	**Pts**
1	Liverpool	42	26	5	11	92	45	57
2	Man United	42	23	7	12	90	62	53
3	Everton	42	21	10	11	84	64	52
4	Tottenham	42	22	7	13	97	81	51
5	Chelsea	42	20	10	12	72	56	50
6	Sheff Wed	42	19	11	12	84	67	49
7	Blackburn	42	18	10	14	89	65	46
8	Arsenal	42	17	11	14	90	82	45
9	Burnley	42	17	10	15	71	64	44
10	West Brom	42	16	11	15	70	61	43
11	Leicester	42	16	11	15	61	58	43
12	Sheff United	42	16	11	15	61	64	43
13	Nottm Forest	42	16	9	17	64	68	41
14	West Ham	42	14	12	16	69	74	40
15	**Fulham**	**42**	**13**	**13**	**16**	**58**	**65**	**39**
16	Wolves	42	12	15	15	70	80	39
17	Stoke	42	14	10	18	77	78	38
18	Blackpool	42	13	9	20	52	73	35
19	Aston Villa	42	11	12	19	62	71	34
20	Birmingham	42	11	7	24	54	92	29
21	Bolton	42	10	8	24	48	80	28
22	Ipswich	42	9	7	26	56	121	25

SEASON 1964-65

DIVISION ONE

The autumn brought many changes both on and off the field. Frank Osborne and Bedford Jezzard, two key men in the club's most successful period going back to 1948, decided to call it a day. Arthur Stevens took over as caretaker manager until Vic Buckingham, a highly regarded tactician, was appointed in January. He was to try to change the character of the club with his ideas, but tradition and history were not responsive to his style.

Back row: Bobby Keetch, Bobby Robson, George Cohen, Tony Macedo, Jimmy Langley, Fred Callaghan; front: Steve Earle, Dave Metchick, Graham Leggat, Johnny Haynes, Brian O'Connell.

After the previous season's solid, and at times exciting, home record, it was almost inevitable that the opening home game should be lost. F.A. Cup winners West Ham kicked off the season with a 2-1 win, ending an unbeaten 14-match run. That apart, the opening results were encouraging. Dave Metchick was finding the net regularly, scoring six times in the first four matches, including a hat-trick against Birmingham City at home. Sadly, it was to prove his swan song, for he joined Leyton Orient mid-way through the season.

Rodney Marsh returned, fully recovered from injury, and finished the season as top scorer with 17 goals. He missed just one League game and produced the sort of form that would, in time, bring him international honours.

England recognition came even sooner for George Cohen, who immediately established himself in Alf Ramsey's England team. The press had also been lobbying for the return of Johnny Haynes, but it had no effect on Ramsey's thinking.

A humiliating defeat at the hands of Fourth Division Millwall in the third round of the Cup underlined a sinking morale, and although new manager Vic Buckingham's first game resulted in a 4-1 win over Nottingham Forest, the expected upturn did not come. As in the previous season, away wins proved elusive. A 3-2 victory at Nottingham Forest in September provided two of the mere nine points won on the club's travels. The Cottagers even managed to lose a two-goal lead at Liverpool in March. Cook and Marsh had put them in a commanding position before slack defending allowed two Callaghan goals to level the scores; Milne's winner in the last minute simply added insult to injury.

F F C
1964-65
DIVISION ONE

With six goals in the first four games of the season, England youth international Dave Metchick started off in sensational style. His best performance was a hat-trick in the 3-1 home win over Birmingham City in midweek. The pictures show two of the goals, both headers, that he scored that night. By October, however, Metchick had lost his place, and by December he was an Orient player.

Manchester United might have snatched a point when they visited the Cottage in September, had not this shot, which beat Macedo, struck a post. Fulham ended up 2-1 winners. By the time the Cottagers travelled to White Hart Lane in October, Marsh had started to score and his confidence was high. He would have a go from any angle, but this effort came to nothing as Spurs won comfortably, 3-0.

MATCH OF THE SEASON
Fulham 5 Leicester City 2
10th October 1964

During the First Division days of the 1960s, Fulham seemed to enjoy playing Leicester. In 16 League meetings between November 1959 and December 1966, the Cottagers won 11 times and drew once. This victory in October 1964 was not only Fulham's best performance of that season, but also their best score against Leicester in that very successful sequence of matches.

For Graham Leggat, the Filberts must have ranked amongst his favourite opponents. He played in 12 of those League encounters, and scored a remarkable 13 goals, including two hat-tricks; he also scored two goals on two other occasions. Every goal, moreover, was put past the great Gordon Banks. He did it again on that autumn day in 1964, watched by a crowd of 14,300; they saw a Fulham team, eighth from the bottom, thrash the visitors, who were eighth from the top. Along with two goals from Leggat (one is shown in the centre picture), came two from Rodney Marsh (top and bottom pictures) and one from Brian O'Connell. Leicester's two, one in each half, were scored by Bobby Roberts, the man bought to replace Frank McLintock, sold a fortnight earlier to Arsenal.

Although few people realised it at the time, this was virtually the end of an era at the Cottage. Within a month, Frank Osborne retired, to be quickly followed by Beddy Jezzard. This opened the way for Vic Buckingham's appointment, and the many changes he would make.

Blackpool shared six goals with Fulham when they visited the Cottage in November. The home side's best goal was a brave header by young Steve Earle, under pressure from international full-back Jimmy Armfield. A month later, Fulham entertained West Brom, the first home game after manager Bedford Jezzard's resignation. With Arthur Stevens in temporary charge, they won 3-1, skipper Haynes getting the third.

In January, Vic Buckingham, a man with impeccable credentials, was appointed manager. Despite his record, however, Fulham's long-term fortunes started to drift downwards about the time of his arrival. A number of Cottage favourites were casualties of his regime, allowed to leave prematurely. These included Jim Langley (pictured supporting the forwards at Highbury in February), Rodney Marsh and Maurice Cook. In the bottom picture, Marsh is No. 8 acknowledging Cook's goal for Fulham against Double-chasing Leeds at the Cottage in March. The game was drawn 2-2, the other goal coming from a Langley penalty (right).

The last victory of the season was against Blackburn on a midweek evening in April at the Cottage. Fulham won 3-2, two of the goals coming from Marsh and Haynes (centre pictures, opposite). Robson got the third. Below right: Maurice Cook challenges the goalkeeper during the visit of Sunderland. Cook scored the only goal in that game, and ended the season second-highest scorer. Few people could have imagined he would have been on his way to Reading that summer after seven years at the Cottage.

Vic Buckingham looks as if he is trying to convince skipper Haynes of the merit of some of his more intricate ideas.

    For an old-fashioned winger, Johnny Key had a respectable scoring record, 37 goals in 187 games, mostly in the top flight. He even got a few with his head, such as against Everton on Easter Monday. This was the penultimate game of the season and ended 1-1.

DIVISION ONE 1964-65 Final League Table

		P	W	D	L	F	A	Pts
1	Man United	42	26	9	7	89	39	61
2	Leeds	42	26	9	7	83	52	61
3	Chelsea	42	24	8	10	89	54	56
4	Everton	42	17	15	10	69	60	49
5	Nottm Forest	42	17	13	12	71	67	47
6	Tottenham	42	19	7	16	87	71	45
7	Liverpool	42	17	10	15	67	73	44
8	Sheff Wed	42	16	11	15	57	55	43
9	West Ham	42	19	4	19	82	71	42
10	Blackburn	42	16	10	16	83	79	42
11	Stoke	42	16	10	16	67	66	42
12	Burnley	42	16	10	16	70	70	42
13	Arsenal	42	17	7	18	69	75	41
14	West Brom	42	13	13	16	70	65	39
15	Sunderland	42	14	9	19	64	74	37
16	Aston Villa	42	16	5	21	57	82	37
17	Blackpool	42	12	11	19	67	78	35
18	Leicester	42	11	13	18	69	85	35
19	Sheff United	42	12	11	19	50	64	35
20	**Fulham**	**42**	**11**	**12**	**19**	**60**	**78**	**34**
21	Wolves	42	13	4	25	59	89	30
22	Birmingham	42	8	11	23	64	96	27

SEASON 1965-66

DIVISION ONE

At the beginning of his first full season at the club, manager Buckingham wrought many changes in personnel. Out went some old favourites, like players Jim Langley and Maurice Cook, as well as Joe Bacuzzi from the back room staff. In came Terry Dyson from Spurs and Mark Pearson from Sheffield Wednesday, unlikely to be the sort of replacements that might steer the club to the greater glories that were being proclaimed in the new, glossy programme. The Hammersmith End

covering that greeted the Fulham faithful was the only tangible evidence that the club was finally moving in the proper direction.

The winning of three points from the opening two matches was one of the few highlights, and two of those points came from a 5-2 home win against a Blackburn side which ended the season at the foot of the table. The campaign that started so optimistically quickly deteriorated into an all too familiar story of survival.

The New Year brought with it the customary early exit from the Cup, and with relegation seemingly unavoidable, the season looked all but over. Changes were made, however. Dave Sexton took over the coaching, youngsters Earle and Barrett came into the side, and McClelland replaced Macedo in goal.

After two close games against London rivals Spurs and Chelsea, a remarkable recovery, even by Fulham's own standards, took place. Liverpool, top of the table, were beaten 2-0 at the Cottage in February, to start an amazing run that yielded 20 points from the remaining 13 games. Allan Clarke, a club record signing from

Back row: Ron Burgess (trainer), Alan Nelmes, Robert Lee, Roger Grant, George Cohen, John Dempsey, Bobby Keetch, Ray Goddard, Tony Macedo, Jack McClelland, Barry Mealand, Bobby Robson, Bobby Drake, Fred Callaghan, Arthur Stevens (trainer); middle row: Geoffrey Heath, Johnny Key, Stan Brown, Graham Leggat, Johnny Haynes, Rodney Marsh, Brian O'Connell, Dave Roberts; front: Lee Adkins, Brian Nichols, Dave Loveridge, John Ryan, Mark Pearson, Terry Parmenter, Jummy Dunkley, Terry Dyson, Tony Goodgame, David Flower, Steve Earle, Dennis Rayner.

Walsall, had to sit it out on the substitute's bench while the goals that he had been bought to score continued to go in.

A 5-2 win at Aston Villa in March gave the Cottagers their first away victory of the season and was the start of five successive away wins that included an important triumph at Elland Road, where few teams won. Survival was all but sealed nine days later at Northampton, where a record crowd witnessed a see-saw match that finished 4-2 to Fulham and ended the Midlands club's only season in the top flight.

There was a trip to the seaside in August to kick off the new season. Manager Vic Buckingham, in his first full season, gives his instructions before the match at Blackpool. Curiously, all the players featured on this page—Macedo and Leggat, Haynes (left, scoring) and Cohen (with Leggat)—were members of the 1958 promotion side. The Cottagers drew 2-2.

F F C
1965-66
DIVISION ONE

A rare headed goal from Stan Brown and a fine shot by Johnny Key, helped the Cottagers beat Blackburn in the first home match of the season. Brown and Key both got second goals in the 5-2 win, the fifth coming from Terry Dyson. Fulham came down to earth with a bump three days later when Chelsea coasted to a 3-0 win at the Cottage. Rodney Marsh found the going tough against Ron Harris.

Fulham found little joy in the visit of Spurs at the begining of September, and lost 0-2. Neither O'Connell nor Marsh could break through. The Cottagers' first hat-trick of the season was scored by Graham Leggat at home to Villa in September. His first goal is shown below. Unfortunately, Villa scored six that day. The best goal in the 3-2 win over Everton (bottom picture) was Mark Pearson's long-range shot.

In an emergency, centre-half John Dempsey was switched to play
centre-forward. He began with a hat-trick in the League Cup against
Northampton. When he scored at Old Trafford (above), a consolation
in a 1-4 defeat in October, it gave him five goals in three games, but he
was soon back in defence.

Goalkeeper Tony Macedo broke his jaw during the Northampton
match in November, and Rodney Marsh was dragooned into the
goalkeeper's jersey (below). In this unfamiliar role, Marsh was unable to
prevent Northampton winning 4-1.

From November onwards, Fulham were struggling and looking like relegation candidates. For once, Gordon Banks had the measure of Graham Leggat, and Leicester cruised to a 5-0 win at Filbert Street, though only a post saved him during the attack shown above. On New Year's Day, however, Arsenal were beaten 1-0 at the Cottage, Bob Wilson having no chance with Leggat's shot. The green shoots of survival peeped through at White Hart Lane. In a narrow 3-4 defeat, Les Barrett scored the first of his 89 goals for Fulham.

Opposite: Leggat got a typical goal at Stamford Bridge (top), in a match Chelsea won 2-1. The tide started to turn, however, when Liverpool were surprisingly beaten 2-0 at the Cottage that same month, February. Steve Earle got both; his first is pictured. This was followed by a 5-2 victory away to Aston Villa (making it 16 goals between them in two League meetings that season). Graham Leggat started the rout with a header after two minutes.

The recovery gathered momentum, and the improbability of escaping relegation started to look a possibility. After Leggat finished off Villa with the fifth goal, Les Barrett sealed a 3-1 win at Upton Park, and then Johnny Haynes put Fulham on the path to victory over West Brom (bottom picture). He also got the second goal in the 2-1 triumph.

Bobby Robson took on the role of penalty taker, which he filled with his customary efficiency. Against Leeds on Good Friday, his goal was a token as the visitors won 3-1. The next week, however, his kick was vital, the fourth in a critical 4-2 win over Sheffield Wednesday.

MATCH OF THE SEASON
Northampton Town 2 Fulham 4
23rd April 1966

In the most improbable and thrilling of all their relegation battles, Fulham virtually clinched another season of First Division football with this win in front of the County Ground's record attendance. After being stranded at the foot of the table for almost four months, Fulham had staged a stunning revival, winning seven out of nine matches. As Fulham travelled up the M1 for this match against the Cobblers, the League positions of the two clubs were such that the losers of the match seemed destined to be relegated along with Blackburn, whilst the winners would almost certainly stay up.

The match was filled with high drama. The home side went ahead after 13 minutes through George Hudson. Bobby Robson put Fulham back on terms after 20 minutes with a looping shot (pictured below). But a few minutes later Robson failed to clear a cross, and Northampton's Joe Kiernan scored with a shot from outside the penalty area to give the home side a 2-1 lead at the interval.

With just 25 minutes of the match left, however, Steve Earle struck with a thrilling hat-trick, the last two goals coming in the final three minutes. His first goal (bottom picture) was whipped in from a great cross by George Cohen, seen at left in the photograph. His second (top opposite) was headed in from a Leggat cross. For his third goal (centre opposite) he ran unchallenged from the half-way line with the Northampton team camped in the Fulham penalty area; he rounded goalkeeper Coe and shot into an empty net.

This victory was followed by one win and two draws in Fulham's last three matches, and the club duly avoided the drop, finishing two points above Northampton who were indeed relegated.

It was a victory and an escape that typified Fulham's First Division existence.

Any lingering worries that, even with the win at Northampton, Fulham might still be relegated were removed three days later when the Cottagers won 2-1 at Nottingham Forest. Both goals came in the first half. Graham Leggat scored the first (top), and the second was scored by Mark Pearson who ended up in the net—and quite delighted! The match was Johnny Haynes' 500th first-team appearance.

		P	W	D	L	F	A	Pts
	DIVISION ONE 1965-66 Final League Table							
1	Liverpool	42	26	9	7	79	34	61
2	Leeds	42	23	9	10	79	38	55
3	Burnley	42	24	7	11	79	47	55
4	Man United	42	18	15	9	84	59	51
5	Chelsea	42	22	7	13	65	53	51
6	West Brom	42	19	12	11	91	69	50
7	Leicester	42	21	7	14	80	65	49
8	Tottenham	42	16	12	14	75	66	44
9	Sheff United	42	16	11	15	56	59	43
10	Stoke	42	15	12	15	65	64	42
11	Everton	42	15	11	16	56	62	41
12	West Ham	42	15	9	18	70	83	39
13	Blackpool	42	14	9	19	55	65	37
14	Arsenal	42	12	13	17	62	75	37
15	Newcastle	42	14	9	19	50	63	37
16	Aston Villa	42	15	6	21	69	80	36
17	Sheff Wed	42	14	8	20	56	66	36
18	Nottm Forest	42	14	8	20	56	72	36
19	Sunderland	42	14	8	20	51	72	36
20	**Fulham**	**42**	**14**	**7**	**21**	**67**	**85**	**35**
21	Northampton	42	10	13	19	55	92	33
22	Blackburn	42	8	4	30	57	88	20

SEASON 1966-67

DIVISION ONE

The season started disappointingly with just two wins in the first two months. Although these early results were less than encouraging, the side nevertheless showed much promise. Manager Vic Buckingham, along with new coach Gordon Jago, brought together a team that combined youth and experience. It was the season when younger players like Clarke, Conway, Barrett, Dempsey and Earle established themselves alongside the more experienced campaigners, such as

Standing: Bobby Robson, Stan Brown, George Cohen, Jack McClelland, John Dempsey, Brian Nichols, Les Barrett; front: Allan Clarke, Steve Earle, Mark Pearson, Johnny Haynes, Graham Leggat.

Cohen, Haynes, Robson and Macedo. In particular, Jimmy Conway, a 19-year-old summer signing from Irish club Bohemians, proved an immediate success. He scored on his debut against Wolves in a League Cup tie, and within weeks made his first appearance for Eire.

But it was Fulham's record signing, Allan Clarke, who was grabbing all the headlines, and his goalscoring feats also brought international recognition. With Earle partnering him up front, the goals started to go in. It was appropriate that Fulham's 2,000th League game against Aston Villa, a 5-1 home win, should signal an upturn in results. Of the next nine games, seven were won, and by the year's end, a mid-table position had been reached. The run included notable victories over title challengers Stoke and a double victory over a strong Leicester City. Transfer-listed Graham Leggat came back into the

attack over Christmas, scoring a hat-trick against Leicester and two more goals against Stoke a few days later. Within days, however, the unsettled Scottish striker was sold to Birmingham City.

Although Fulham were always capable of producing form equal to any team in the division, they were unable to do so on a regular basis. It was this lack of consistency that prevented a higher placing than the 18th they finally achieved. It was a source of great frustration that the team which could match and at times better the likes of Manchester United and Liverpool should have in the end so little to show for all their efforts.

FFC
1966-67
DIVISION ONE

In spite of losing their first two games, Fulham survived quite comfortably in Division One in 1966-67. It looked like three defeats on the trot as the Cottagers trailed 0-1 at Stoke with only 15 minutes to go. Then Graham Leggat and Allan Clarke struck to secure both points (pictures left). Clarke with 24 goals, and Steve Earle with 12, dominated the scoring list that season. Earle was on the mark in a 1-5 defeat at West Brom (bottom left) and at Newcastle in a 1-1 draw in September (above). The following month, Fulham travelled to Anfield and Allan Clarke caught the eye with both goals in a 2-2 draw.

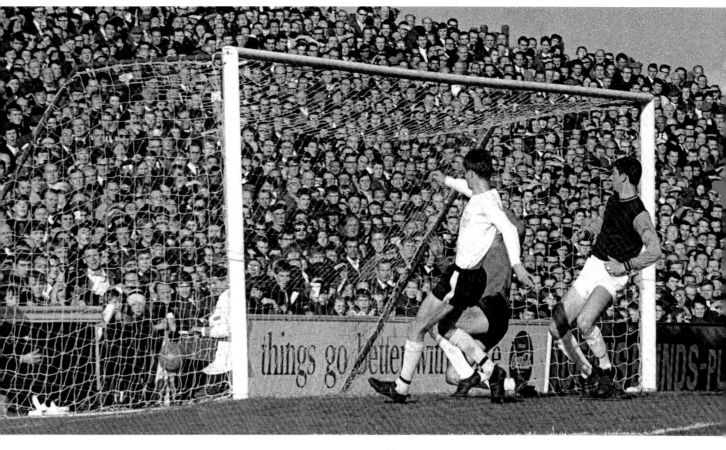

That man Clarke played a big part in two of the best wins of the season, a 4-2 success over West Ham in October and a 5-1 thrashing handed out to Aston Villa in November. Against the Hammers, he touched in Fulham's third from inside the six-yard box; this was his second goal of the match. He also scored twice against Villa, including this dramatic third goal for Fulham, superbly headed in from a cross by Barrett (at right in the picture).

F^FC
1966-67
DIVISION ONE

Opposite page: In December, when five of six games were won, other players were queuing up, as they say, to get their share of the limelight. Jimmy Conway found the net in the 3-1 home win over Southampton; Steve Earle got the only goal of the game at Blackpool; whilst Fred Callaghan and Les Barrett won the points at Leicester.

An old favourite signed off in style in the last two games of 1966. Graham
Leggat, back in the side for the visit of Leicester City, scored a marvellous
hat-trick in the 4-2 win. His three goals are shown opposite. The scoring was
completed by a goal from Haynes (above) with a fierce long-range drive.
Four days later Stoke were at the Cottage, the side against which Leggat had
made his Fulham debut in 1958. From 0-1 down, the Cottagers came back to
win 4-1. Graham scored twice, but today would probably be credited with a
third. Fulham's second goal (below), came from his shot which cannoned off
defender Skeels into the net. Leggat's official second goal—and his last for the
club—is shown at the foot of the page. Days later, manager Buckingham
sold Fulham's most prolific goalscorer to Birmingham for a paltry £15,000.

The home game with West Brom in January 1967 was drawn 2-2. Ted Drake's son, Bobby, made a rare appearance at full-back, but the afternoon was more notable for the failure of the floodlights.

Steve Earle was becoming an increasingly mature and effective striker. He contributed a splendid headed goal to the 5-1 win over Newcastle in February, and scored with a well-placed shot at the Dell, where Southampton won 4-2.

MATCH OF THE SEASON
Fulham 2 Manchester United 2
27th March 1967

For once, relegation was not a serious threat to Fulham, and the Easter Monday crowd, of 47,290, the second largest ever at the Cottage, came to see League leaders Manchester United try to strengthen their grip on the title race. With Best, Law and Charlton in their line-up, United were the country's top attraction, but on the day, they met their match and were grateful for a share of the spoils.

It was a thrilling see-saw encounter. In the first 15 minutes, Fulham ran United ragged and had a number of good efforts on goal, such as Barrett's, above. They deservedly took the lead when Clarke headed in Haynes' free-kick (right). United fought back and Aston hit the bar, and it was no surprise when they equalised. Law fed Best who went past Dempsey to shoot beyond Macedo. In the second half, Fulham regained the initiative and took the lead with a stunning

Barrett goal (below), a result of a sweeping move involving Cohen, Haynes and Pearson. Victory was denied the Cottagers with a late equaliser by Stiles, and in the dying minutes, United could have won.

This was an epic encounter where the honours were quite rightly shared.

The return match at Old Trafford against Manchester United took place the day after the home encounter. It was watched by almost 52,000 people. Fulham lost 1-2, but the headlines next day focussed on goalkeeper Ian Seymour's splendid debut for the Cottagers. Below: The dismissal of Allan Clarke and Ian Ure was the most memorable feature of the last occasion that Fulham took a League point from Arsenal; the match, in April 1967, ended in a goalless draw.

Whilst Clarke's and Earle's goalscoring exploits tended to grab the headlines, the quiet efficiency of ever-present John Dempsey made a major contribution to the defence. Against Arsenal at the Cottage, he shows George Graham (No. 9) who's boss.

DIVISION ONE 1966-67 Final League Table

		P	W	D	L	F	A	Pts
1	Man United	42	24	12	6	84	45	60
2	Nottm Forest	42	23	10	9	64	41	56
3	Tottenham	42	24	8	10	71	48	56
4	Leeds	42	22	11	9	62	42	55
5	Liverpool	42	19	13	10	64	47	51
6	Everton	42	19	10	13	65	46	48
7	Arsenal	42	16	14	12	58	47	46
8	Leicester	42	18	8	16	78	71	44
9	Chelsea	42	15	14	13	67	62	44
10	Sheff United	42	16	10	16	52	59	42
11	Sheff Wed	42	14	13	15	56	47	41
12	Stoke	42	17	7	18	63	58	41
13	West Brom	42	16	7	19	77	73	39
14	Burnley	42	15	9	18	66	76	39
15	Man City	42	12	15	15	43	52	39
16	West Ham	42	14	8	20	80	84	36
17	Sunderland	42	14	8	20	58	72	36
18	**Fulham**	**42**	**11**	**12**	**19**	**71**	**83**	**34**
19	Southampton	42	14	6	22	74	92	34
20	Newcastle	42	12	9	21	39	81	33
21	Aston Villa	42	11	7	24	54	85	29
22	Blackpool	42	6	9	27	41	76	21

SEASON 1967-68

DIVISION ONE

After nine years in the First Division, the fight for survival was finally lost. The season started poorly and got progressively worse. Allan Clarke continued to score goals, but defensively the team was consistently vulnerable, and for most of the season the side remained in the bottom two positions in the table. Vic Buckingham tried to give youth a chance. Forward Bobby Moss and Ian Seymour, a brave and fearless 19-year-old goalkeeper, came in to make up one of Fulham's youngest ever sides. The team showed on occasions the flair that players such as Barrett, Clarke and

Back row: Barry Mealand, John Dempsey, Allan Clarke, John Ryan, Jimmy Houliston; standing: Gordon Jago (coach), Steve Earle, Bobby Drake, Jack McClelland, Tony Macedo, Ian Seymour, Brian Nichols, Mike Pentecost, Arthur Stevens (trainer), Eric Mardling (physio); seated: Hugh Cunningham, Fred Callaghan, Johnny Haynes, Stan Brown, George Cohen, Turlough O'Connor, Jimmy Conway, Terry Parmenter; front: Les Barrett, Mark Pearson, Terry Dyson, Bobby Moss.

Conway amongst others undoubtedly had. New signing from Clyde, Joe Gilroy, provided fresh impetus that brought an undefeated run throughout November, including a quarter-final place in the League Cup. A 1-1 draw against Liverpool at the beginning of December was marred by a serious injury to captain George Cohen. It was a loss that the team could ill afford, and the hoped-for revival faltered.

The New Year opened with successive home defeats by Leeds and Leicester, and the inevitable departure of manager Vic Buckingham. Bobby Robson returned from a brief appointment in the North American League to take charge. A fortunate win against non-League Macclesfield Town in the F.A. Cup couldn't hide the enormity of his task. It was duly emphasised in the next game, a 7-2 thrashing at West Ham.

Defensive problems prompted Bobby Robson to sign Reg Matthewson from Sheffield United. It had little effect, and goals were still being conceded at an alarming rate. With time running out, ex-England forward Johnny Byrne was signed to partner Allan Clarke up front. It proved to be a hasty purchase; Byrne, past his best, sustained an injury after just four games. With three games remaining, the fight against relegation was finally lost when Stoke City, also in danger, travelled to the Cottage and won 2-0.

F^FC
1967-68
DIVISION ONE

From the start of the season, Fulham's grip on their First Division status
looked precarious. Sunderland were beaten at the Cottage 3-2 by a late
Haynes winner (that's him celebrating, above centre), and Everton were
overcome 2-1; but these were isolated successes. In the Everton match,
Barrett scored the first (left), and young Bobby Moss (No.8) got the dramatic
winner (below) in the last minute. However, more typical of the season was
a defeat at Leeds (top left), where Jack Charlton kept a grip on Les Barrett.

During their First Division years, Leicester was one of Fulham's favourite
haunts. They won there again in September 1968, Haynes heading in the
winner (above). But this win ushered in a run of six successive defeats.

Joe Gilroy was bought from Clyde to strengthen the attack. In the picture, left, he follows Allan Clarke's header into the Forest net for the Cottagers'—and Clarke's—second goal in a 2-0 home win in November. This was followed by a surprise 1-0 win at Stoke, Haynes getting the vital goal.

F F C
1967-68
DIVISION ONE

A great goal by Bobby Moss (No. 8) at Molineux in December (above) raised hopes of at least a point, but Wolves ran out 3-2 winners. Vic Buckingham's last game in charge was at home to Leicester, and the 0-1 defeat, in which neither Earle nor Conway could make much headway, confirmed Fulham's position as relegation favourites.

In January, Bobby Robson was back at the Cottage for his third spell, the first two as a player and this time as manager. His first League match at the helm started encouragingly when Allan Clarke put Fulham ahead at Upton Park. Steve Earle got a second, but unfortunately West Ham scored seven. In the picture above, Joe Gilroy came close to narrowing the deficit, but the cause was forlorn. In the next match, at home to Burnley, Robson witnessed Gilroy being stretchered off with an injury that would keep him out of the side for two months. The Burnley match is featured opposite.

MATCH OF THE SEASON
Fulham 4 Burnley 3
10th February 1968

After so many near misses, the First Division relegation trap-door finally opened for Fulham at the end of this season. A dreadful run of results from the turn of the year left the club adrift at the foot of the table, and led to the departure of manager Vic Buckingham. This was the first League win under new manager Bobby Robson. Though thoroughly deserved, it did not spark another heroic revival.

Fulham had Reg Matthewson making his debut after his move from Sheffield United, but suffered the loss of Joe Gilroy with an ankle injury just before half-time. Gilroy was replaced by John Ryan (right). By then, the Cottagers led 1-0 through Earle who headed home a Haynes free-kick (above). Burnley came back on the hour with two goals in a minute, from Lochhead and Casper, but Fulham clawed their way back thanks to a goal by Allan Clarke after 74 minutes. The turning-point came with nine minutes to go, when Haynes, in a suspiciously offside position, fired in after the ball had been deflected by a Burnley defender (picture below). With only seconds left, Clarke made the game safe when he converted Callaghan's cross, and although Dempsey put through his own goal with virtually the last kick of the afternoon, Fulham picked up their first win in nine League matches. Sadly, there were just three more wins to come in the remaining 16 First Division games.

Unlike previous seasons, Fulham went down with a whimper. There were, however, isolated moments of quality, such as Earle's superb lob which clinched the 2-0 home win over Sheffield Wednesday in February, and Clarke's opportunist effort at Maine Road, where eventual League champions Manchester City strolled to a 5-1 victory.

The best of Steve Earle was still to come,
but he showed glimpses of his class in a
dismal season, such as this headed goal in
a 1-1 home draw with Coventry.

Allan Clarke attracted the attention of
First Division managers with his 27 goals
in a season of struggle; his goal at
Nottingham Forest in April was a fine
individual effort (below).

Joe Gilroy had most of what a top
striker needed, except luck. This miss
against Newcastle (bottom picture) was,
nevertheless, unimportant, as Fulham won
2-0, their last home win in Division One.

Fulham's last win in the top flight was at Bramall Lane, where
they came back from 0-2 down against Sheffield United with
three goals in the last 20 minutes. Les Barrett got the equaliser
(top picture).

A trip to Anfield is always a daunting prospect, and in
April, Liverpool won 4-1. The Cottagers' goal, almost
inevitably, came from Allan Clarke, his 57th—and last—in
two years.

		P	W	D	L	F	A	Pts
	DIVISION ONE 1967-68 Final League Table							
1	Man City	42	26	6	10	86	43	58
2	Man United	42	24	8	10	89	55	56
3	Liverpool	42	22	11	9	71	40	55
4	Leeds	42	22	9	11	71	41	53
5	Everton	42	23	6	13	67	40	52
6	Chelsea	42	18	12	12	62	68	48
7	Tottenham	42	19	9	14	70	59	47
8	West Brom	42	17	12	13	75	62	46
9	Arsenal	42	17	10	15	60	56	44
10	Newcastle	42	13	15	14	54	67	41
11	Nottm Forest	42	14	11	17	52	64	39
12	West Ham	42	14	10	18	73	69	38
13	Leicester	42	13	12	17	64	69	38
14	Burnley	42	14	10	18	64	71	38
15	Sunderland	42	13	11	18	51	61	37
16	Southampton	42	13	11	18	66	83	37
17	Wolves	42	14	8	20	66	75	36
18	Stoke	42	14	7	21	50	73	35
19	Sheff Wed	42	11	12	19	51	63	34
20	Coventry	42	9	15	18	51	71	33
21	Sheff United	42	11	10	21	49	70	32
22	**Fulham**	**42**	**10**	**7**	**25**	**56**	**98**	**27**

Season 1968-69

DIVISION TWO

Any thoughts of an immediate return to the First Division were quickly dispelled. Early season results showed no improvement from the previous term, and, following Allan Clarke's British record transfer to Leicester, the goals soon dried up. Frank Large, a much travelled goalscorer, joined as part of the deal, but proved to be an unlucky and disappointing replacement. Full-back Malcolm Macdonald was tried at centre-forward and was an unlikely but immediate success, scoring

Standing: Bobby Robson (manager), Reg Matthewson, Fred Callaghan, George Cohen, Ian Seymour, Tony Macedo, Jack McClelland, John Dempsey, Jimmy Conway; front: Stan Brown, Joe Gilroy, Johnny Haynes, Johnny Byrne, Frank Large, John Ryan, Steve Earle, Les Barrett.

five goals in eight starts. He was unable to keep his place, however; Bobby Robson preferred instead to include recent signings Vic Halom from Orient and Cliff Jones from Spurs.

In early November, with only two games won, Bobby Robson was sacked, just ten months after taking control. Johnny Haynes took temporary charge, but 17 days later resigned, making way for Bill Dodgin's appointment as the new manager. Apart from a 2-0 win at home to Birmingham City on Boxing Day, results failed to improve. More new signings were made. Wilf Tranter, Brian Dear and Stan Horne joined another newcomer, Barry Lloyd, who came from Chelsea as part of an exchange that took John Dempsey to Stamford Bridge. By the season's end, a total of 31 players had been tried. Undoubtedly, the best performances came in the F.A. Cup, against two First Division sides. Sunderland were beaten 4-1 away in the third round, before Fulham went out in the next round, a narrow defeat at the Cottage by the holders West Brom.

George Cohen, unable to regain full fitness, decided to retire, and played his last game at Bristol City at the beginning of March. A brief winning run during that month brought victories against promotion hopefuls Millwall and Cardiff, but it was never going to be enough to prevent relegation for the second successive year.

The season was one of the worst on record, a fact reflected in matchday attendances, with the average crowd 8,000 down on the previous season. The many changes in players and personnel never permitted a settled side, and, not surprisingly, just seven games were won throughout. The points total, 25, was the lowest in the club's history.

F^FC
1968-69
DIVISION TWO

Goals were in extremely short supply when Fulham dropped back into the Second Division. A goal by Conway at Blackpool in September (picture top left; Conway is not in the photo) was only the fourth in ten League matches. A reserve full-back, Malcolm Macdonald, was tried in desperation at centre-forward at Oxford (left), and although he did not score then, he began to make his mark. The visit of Portsmouth to the Cottage in November marked Bobby Robson's last home game in charge, and John Dempsey's goal (bottom left) in a 2-2 draw was Fulham's last in his short reign.

Macdonald was the find of the season who went on to great things—with other clubs. On Friday the 13th (of September), Macdonald ended the club's goalscoring drought, which had lasted 660 minutes, with his debut goal that won the game against Crystal Palace (above). He went on to score in four of Fulham's next six games, before losing his place. In the picture below, he races through against Blackburn, watched by his striking partner, Frank Large, who had joined Fulham as part of the deal that took Clarke to Leicester. Large, enthusiastic but unlucky, took 12 matches to register his first goal.

MATCH OF THE SEASON
Fulham 4 Huddersfield Town 3
23rd November 1968

In a season characterised by lows rather than highs, this match and result stand apart from the rest. In the late autumn of 1968, the club was pretty much in disarray. Relegated from Division One the previous year, Fulham had drifted down towards the foot of Division Two. They had failed to score in half of their 18 League games before the visit of the Terriers and had sacked manager Bobby Robson the previous week.

Johnny Haynes stepped up to become acting player-manager and inspired the side to a thrilling victory. With two minutes gone, however, another defeat seemed on the cards, when a bad back pass by Stan Brown led to Lawson opening the scoring for Huddersfield. However, Haynes created an equaliser for Byrne, his first goal for Fulham (top picture), and he then set up Conway for a second before half-time. Although Lawson equalised in the 60th minute, goals from Vic Halom (above) and Cliff Jones (right) gave the Cottagers the comfort of a two-goal margin before Paul Aimson ended the scoring in the dying minutes.

Cliff Jones had been a dynamic
winger for Spurs, and he joined
Fulham in October. Despite
wholehearted effort, such as here at
Middlesbrough, he was unable to
revive Fulham's fortunes.
   After Bobby Robson's departure in
November, and Johnny Haynes' brief
interregnum, Bill Dodgin returned to
the Cottage for a third spell (1949
and 1961 were the previous
occasions), but this time as manager.
His father had held the post between
1949 and 1953.

There were still one or two players who knew where the goal was. Malcolm Macdonald scored what proved to be his final goal for Fulham, at home in the 1-3 defeat by Norwich in October, and in December Les Barrett scored what might have been his best goal, against Cardiff, though this was in another defeat, this time 1-5.

Opposite page: Even when Fulham managed to get three goals at Charlton in November, their opponents got five. For John Ryan, the game marked his first ever goal in League football. In the picture of his goal (top), John is at the left.

The second of Vic Halom's 25 goals in 82 outings for Fulham came in a 2-0 home win over Birmingham on Boxing Day.

There were plenty of tense moments in the Fulham goalmouth that season. At Portsmouth in January, Fred Callaghan came to the rescue of goalkeeper Brian Williamson, but the Cottagers still lost, 1-3.

As the Third Division beckoned, there was a flurry of activity on the transfer market. Several were panic buys, but Barry Lloyd proved a shrewd acquisition. His first goal for the club (top) was in his third game, at home to Preston. He also scored the other goal in the 2-0 win.

Les Barrett managed only two goals all season. In the picture above, he is seen turning two Millwall defenders inside out, and he managed to score in the 2-0 victory that day in March. But it was the last home win of a dreadful season. Les was one of only seven of the 31 players used that season who were still to be regulars when Fulham next played in Division Two in 1971-72.

	DIVISION TWO	**1968-69**		**Final League Table**				
		P	W	D	L	F	A	Pts
1	Derby	42	26	11	5	65	32	63
2	Crystal Palace	42	22	12	8	70	47	56
3	Charlton	42	18	14	10	61	52	50
4	Middlesbrough	42	19	11	12	58	49	49
5	Cardiff	42	20	7	15	67	54	47
6	Huddersfield	42	17	12	13	53	46	46
7	Birmingham	42	18	8	16	73	59	44
8	Blackpool	42	14	15	13	51	41	43
9	Sheff United	42	16	11	15	61	50	43
10	Millwall	42	17	9	16	57	49	43
11	Hull	42	13	16	13	59	52	42
12	Carlisle	42	16	10	16	46	49	42
13	Norwich	42	15	10	17	53	56	40
14	Preston	42	12	15	15	38	44	39
15	Portsmouth	42	12	14	16	58	58	38
16	Bristol City	42	11	16	15	46	53	38
17	Bolton	42	12	14	16	55	67	38
18	Aston Villa	42	12	14	16	37	48	38
19	Blackburn	42	13	11	18	52	63	37
20	Oxford	42	12	9	21	34	55	33
21	Bury	42	11	8	23	51	80	30
22	**Fulham**	**42**	**7**	**11**	**24**	**40**	**81**	**25**

Season 1969-70

DIVISION THREE

The slide down the Football League was at last checked. Early season performances were not only encouraging in terms of points but also entertaining, and the goals that had been so sadly lacking in the previous season started to flow. These came from a new look forward line of Steve Earle, Les Barrett and Jimmy Conway. With an attack a cut above the Third Division norm, games were won convincingly—including a record-breaking 8-0 victory at Halifax. But the hoped-for promotion push faltered at the beginning of October. Just one win in a 13-match run saw the team drop into the

Back row: Wilf Tranter, Reg Matthewson, Vic Halom, Brian Williamson, Ian Seymour, Dave Roberts, John Gilchrist, Danny O'Leary; centre: Steve Earle, Johnny Haynes, Stan Brown, Stan Horne, Jimmy Conway, Cliff Jones, Frank Large; front: Barry Lloyd, Mike Pentecost, Les Barrett, Fred Callaghan, Dave Moreline.

bottom half of the table. Malcolm Webster, bought from Arsenal, replaced Seymour in goal, and did much to steady the defence and in turn raise team morale. Johnny Haynes, in his 19th season at the club, was playing as well as ever. But it was sadly his last, and he played his final game in a home match against Stockport County in January. It was ironic that in his absence the team's results began to improve.

The second half of the season was played out in true promotion style. Just three games were lost in 22, which enabled the Cottagers to close the gap on the leaders. But the revival came too late to give Fulham any realistic chance of catching the top clubs, Luton and Orient. It was Luton who finally put an end to any lingering hopes

that Fulham had of promotion when they went to the Cottage and won with a goal scored by ex-Fulham player Malcolm Macdonald. There was, however, the consolation of finishing the season as one of the Division's highest scorers, thus qualifying for the Watney Cup the following August.

Back in the Third Division after 37 years, Fulham began rather tentatively. The first win did not come until the third game, at home to Gillingham. The Cottagers took the lead through Haynes—his first goal in the Third Division, and the one which took him past Bedford Jezzard's record. It needed a penalty, converted by Conway, to win the match, however. Haynes and Brown (left) are in no doubt about the offence.

Conway and Earle were emerging as a potent strike force. Both were on the mark at Eastville in September, Conway with the first (above), but Bristol Rovers won 3-2. John Richardson went close to equalising with a header (below).

MATCH OF THE SEASON
Fulham 4 Plymouth Argyle 3
20th September 1969

The outstanding result in this first season back in Division Three for 37 years was the record 8-0 away win at Halifax. There was, however, no photographer on duty that evening, and so the choice for match of the season falls on the thrilling home game against Plymouth that took place four days later.

Not surprisingly, the same players who had crushed Halifax took the field against the Pilgrims, and the result could so easily have been the same. This time, it was Jimmy Conway rather than Steve Earle who was the star. He set up Barry Lloyd for Fulham's equaliser (top picture) after a Stan Horne own goal had given the visitors the lead, and then he scored himself before the interval (above). Haynes, who a month earlier had passed Jezzard's club scoring record, made it 3-1 (right), and a cricket score looked a real possibility. Like many of Bill Dodgin Junior's teams, however, an emphasis on attack led to carelessness in defence, and Plymouth came back into the game through Reynolds and Bickle. The seventh and deciding goal came inevitably from Conway, who took his season's tally to 12 in 12 games.

Stan Brown was almost prolific as a goal-scorer in the autumn of 1969. His headed equaliser against Doncaster at home in October (he is No. 2 in the picture, above left) was his second of the season, his best tally for four years.

Despite being surrounded by Bournemouth defenders at Dean Court the same month, Steve Earle heads home a typically fine goal.

F F C
1969-70
DIVISION THREE

Both Earle and Conway scored over 20 goals in 1969-70, many of which were set up by Les Barrett's bursts down the wing and tantalising crosses. Here he flies past a floundering Brighton defender.

In January, Fulham made a late bid to join the promotion contenders. A 3-1 win at Walsall, sealed by Steve Earle's 20-yard shot, started the surge from mid-table which ended two places short of promotion.

F^FC

FFC
1969-70
DIVISION THREE

Substitute and defender John Gilchrist
scored the equalising goal (top) in a 3-3
thriller at Barnsley in February. There were
three more goals against a Yorkshire club
the following week—at home to
Rotherham—and these were worth two
points. Even Ken Coton's wide-angle lens
could not get scorer Barry Lloyd and the
goal in the picture for the opening strike
(above), but it was easier when Vic Halom
finished off Conway's cross from 12 yards,
for Fulham's second goal.

Promotion hopes were kept alive when Reading were beaten 4-0 at Elm Park in March, Fulham's fourth consecutive win. Two of the goals came from a Halom header (top) and an Earle shot (above). Away again a few days later, at Torquay, Les Barrett was on hand to open the scoring (below), but United equalised in the second half.

Still in with a mathematical chance of going up on Easter Monday, Fulham scored four (or more) goals in a match for the sixth time that season, when Brighton were the visitors to the Cottage. Vic Halom (No. 8) started the victory march, getting on the end of Conway's cross, and Conway finished it with a penalty.

DIVISION THREE 1969-70 Final League Table

		P	W	D	L	F	A	Pts
1	Orient	46	25	12	9	67	36	62
2	Luton	46	23	14	9	77	43	60
3	Bristol Rovers	46	20	16	10	80	59	56
4	**Fulham**	**46**	**20**	**15**	**11**	**81**	**55**	**55**
5	Brighton	46	23	9	14	57	43	55
6	Mansfield	46	21	11	14	70	49	53
7	Barnsley	46	19	15	12	68	59	53
8	Reading	46	21	11	14	87	77	53
9	Rochdale	46	18	10	18	69	60	46
10	Bradford City	46	17	12	17	57	50	46
11	Doncaster	46	17	12	17	52	54	46
12	Walsall	46	17	12	17	54	67	46
13	Torquay	46	14	17	15	62	59	45
14	Rotherham	46	15	14	17	62	54	44
15	Shrewsbury	46	13	18	15	62	63	44
16	Tranmere	46	14	16	16	56	72	44
17	Plymouth	46	16	11	19	56	64	43
18	Halifax	46	14	15	17	47	63	43
19	Bury	46	15	11	20	75	80	41
20	Gillingham	46	13	13	20	52	64	39
21	Bournemouth	46	12	15	19	48	71	39
22	Southport	46	14	10	22	48	66	38
23	Barrow	46	8	14	24	46	81	30
24	Stockport	46	6	11	29	27	71	23

SEASON 1970-71

DIVISION THREE

Not since 1958-59, when promotion was last won, had the club started a season so well. Fulham rightly confirmed their position as promotion favourites by heading the table from the opening day. Early results raised supporters' expectations, none more so than the 5-0 home thrashing of Bradford City. Each of the forwards, Earle, Conway, Barrett, Halom and Lloyd, scored in a thoroughly convincing win. Barry Lloyd took over from the departed Johnny Haynes as both captain and 'play-maker', an unenviable task but one in which he would soon revel. Although the emphasis

was on attack, manager Bill Dodgin spent £18,000 on Jimmy Dunne, a polished defender from Torquay, who could also play in midfield.

Success also came in the Football League Cup. Wins against Second Division clubs Orient, QPR and Swindon earned Fulham a place in the quarter-finals for only the second time.

A slump in form in November and December coincided with an injury to winger Jimmy Conway who, along with his fellow forwards, was at times a target for some questionable tactics from the opposition. This apart, Fulham led the Division for much of the season, never dropping lower than fourth place. An important win away to Bristol Rovers, themselves challenging for promotion, was followed by three home victories and a return to the top of the table.

Promotion was secured in the penultimate match, away at Bradford City. George Johnston, an early

Back row: Bill Dodgin (manager), Dave Robertson, Stan Horne, Jimmy Dunne, John Richardson, Ian Seymour, Malcolm Webster, Dave Moreline, Dave Roberts, Fred Callaghan, Wilf Tranter, George Cohen (youth coach), Terry Medwin (coach); centre: Reg Matthewson, Mike Pentecost, Jimmy Conway, Barry Lloyd, Steve Earle, Vic Halom, Les Barrett, Stan Brown; front: John Brickell, John Graham, McAndrew Johnson, Tommy James, John Fraser.

season buy from Birmingham City, got the all important goal in the 3-2 win. Fulham went into the last game, against Preston North End, needing just a single point to win the Third Division championship. With home advantage and in front of the largest home crowd of the season, 25,774, Fulham failed to secure the point they needed, losing 1-0 to a Preston side which a few days later won their remaining game to pip Fulham to the title. It was a disappointing end to what was an otherwise successful campaign.

If all that came out of the first home match of the season against Swansea was this photograph of a Steve Earle goal, it would still have been memorable. As a bonus, Halom, Dunne, and Earle again, added to the scoring in the 4-1 win. The impressive start to the season continued when Bradford City were crushed 5-0 at the Cottage, making it three wins in four games. Jimmy Conway opened his account for the season with the fourth.

F^FC

1970-71
DIVISION THREE

Opposite page: Conway was again on the mark (top) when Doncaster travelled to SW6 in September, a match which finished 1-1. The fact that the side scored 68 League goals that season tends to obscure the contribution made by the solid defence. Reg Matthewson, shown dispossessing a Doncaster player, was a model of consistency at the back. For once, Fulham won points regularly away from home, even on difficult trips such as to Rochdale in September. The decider in the 2-1 victory came from Les Barrett who fastened on the the rebound when Earle's shot was blocked.

F^FC
1970-71
DIVISION THREE

Brighton and Tranmere left the
Cottage empty-handed in September.
The Seagulls, who were later to be
managed by Barry Lloyd, lost to the
Fulham skipper's long-range shot
(top), whilst Rovers conceded a goal
to Vic Halom. The other picture
illustrates the conflict between love
and duty, as a cameraman prefers to
watch the match rather than
photograph it—always a difficult
decision.

106

Steve Earle, who had scored five at Halifax the previous season, was restricted to one goal (top)—the third in a 3-1 win—when the Yorkshire club visited the Cottage in October. When Fulham travelled to Yorkshire in November, they had to settle for a point at Rotherham, thanks to George Johnston's goal. By February, when Fulham met Port Vale at home, they were in third place. Les Barrett's goal after 75 seconds set them up for an emphatic 4-0 win.

Torquay were hit for four at the Cottage in February. Although noted for Reg Matthewson's only goal in his 174 games for Fulham, it was Les Barrett's goal, the first of the four, which was the best. By March, nerves were getting a bit frayed, and all the experience of the likes of Steve Earle was vital. His shot against Rotherham clinched both points.

F F C

1970-71
DIVISION THREE

Opposite page: In the closing weeks, vital wins were secured over Walsall at home (1-0), and at Gillingham (3-1) and Doncaster (1-0). Les Barrett did the damage to the Saddlers; he also put the match at Priestfield beyond doubt, but it was Steve Earle who was the match winner at Doncaster.

MATCH OF THE SEASON
Bradford City 2   Fulham 3
28th April 1971

Fulham's two-year sojourn in the Third Division ended with this hard-earned midweek victory at Valley Parade. Rarely out of the top two all season, the Cottagers clinched promotion with one game to spare.

Fielding the side which had found its best form in the final three months of the season,

Fulham dominated the early play. Earle, Barrett and Conway all missed chances before George Johnston put the visitors ahead after 32 minutes (above). Bradford snatched a surprise equaliser on half-time through John Hall, but a lob by skipper Barry Lloyd after 55 minutes (below) restored the Cottagers' advantage. Again City came back, this time from a Norman Corner header, only for Johnston to strike yet again (opposite), with a great header just

15 minutes from time, to secure the points and promotion. Afterwards, in the dressing room, champagne magically appeared, and in the picture Bill Dodgin is pouring a spot for Stan Horne, while directer Chappie D'Amato looks on with great delight.

The win left Fulham to face Preston three days later at the Cottage needing just a point to collect their second divisional title. Rather predictably, they lost 0-1, and had to settle for runners-up spot.

Players and wives celebrate the return to Division Two, whilst chairman Tommy Trinder looks understandably pleased and proud.

DIVISION THREE 1970-71 Final League Table

		P	W	D	L	F	A	Pts
1	Preston	46	22	17	7	63	39	61
2	**Fulham**	46	24	12	10	68	41	60
3	Halifax	46	22	12	12	74	55	56
4	Aston Villa	46	19	15	12	54	46	53
5	Chesterfield	46	17	17	12	66	38	51
6	Bristol Rovers	46	19	13	14	69	50	51
7	Mansfield	46	18	15	13	64	62	51
8	Rotherham	46	17	16	13	64	60	50
9	Wrexham	46	18	13	15	72	65	49
10	Torquay	46	19	11	16	54	57	49
11	Swansea	46	15	16	15	59	56	46
12	Barnsley	46	17	11	18	49	52	45
13	Shrewsbury	46	16	13	17	58	62	45
14	Brighton	46	14	16	16	50	47	44
15	Plymouth	46	12	19	15	63	63	43
16	Rochdale	46	14	15	17	61	68	43
17	Port Vale	46	15	12	19	52	59	42
18	Tranmere	46	10	22	14	45	55	42
19	Bradford City	46	13	14	19	49	62	40
20	Walsall	46	14	11	21	51	57	39
21	Reading	46	14	11	21	48	85	39
22	Bury	46	12	13	21	52	60	37
23	Doncaster	46	13	9	24	45	66	35
24	Gillingham	46	10	13	23	42	67	33

Season 1971-72

DIVISION TWO

After a bright start, Fulham remained for most of the season in danger of a quick return to the Third Division. All in all, it was a disappointing campaign for the club after the exciting way in which promotion had been won the previous season. A convincing 3-0 home win against Watford opened the season, but it was six long weeks before even another goal was scored. Despite the construction of a new £250,000 stand on the river side of the ground, the fans were becoming

increasingly frustrated, preferring to see cash spent on the team instead. A signing was made, though, when striker Roger Cross was bought from Brentford to replace Vic Halom who had joined Luton Town. But it was the return of Jimmy Conway from injury that sparked a brief revival. Six wins in October and November hoisted the team into a mid-table position, but it was not to last, and by the turn of the year Fulham had dropped back into relegation danger. In an attempt to tighten up the defence, goalkeeper Peter Mellor was signed from Burnley, to replace Malcolm Webster.

The better performances were reserved for games where no points were at stake. In the F.A. Cup, a strong QPR side was beaten 2-1 after a replay. The new Riverside Stand was officially opened with a prestigious game against Portuguese champions, Benfica. Again Fulham belied their League form and played some splendid football, deservedly winning 3-2.

In the League, however, the club were still struggling near the bottom of the table, and they turned to old boy Alan Mullery, who came on loan from Tottenham Hotspur. It was a move that provoked an angry outburst from fellow relegation candidates, accusing the London clubs of the 'old pals act'. Although his stay was short, just six games, his inspiration was a major factor, helping to achieve home wins against Sheffield Wednesday (4-0) and Millwall (1-0). The season's most significant result, however, came in early April away to a team also in trouble, Charlton. It was only a late headed goal by Fred Callaghan that gave the Cottagers a share of the points. It proved to be an important equaliser, for it helped Fulham to secure their Second Division status by just one point. Ironically, the last relegation place was taken by Charlton.

F F
C
1971-72
DIVISION TWO

An impressive 3-0 win over Watford in the Cottagers' first game back in Division Two flattered only to deceive. On that day, however, it was goalkeeper Mike Walker who was deceived by Steve Earle's rasping drive, and the photograph (top left) was of as high a quality as the goal. There then followed six games in which Fulham failed to score, but defender Reg Matthewson nearly ended the goal drought (left) with a last-minute header at Swindon that was cleared off the line. In the end, it was Les Barrett who broke the barren spell with a goal in the 2-1 home victory over Orient at the end of September.

When Hull were beaten 1-0 at the Cottage in October, it was only the third win in 11 League matches, and of the six goals scored, Earle had got four, including the winner (above) against the Tigers. At Fratton Park later that month, Fulham scored three times, but unfortunately for them, Portsmouth got six. Conway (No. 7) scored the first two, his second squeezed in from a narrow angle.

A home win over Blackpool at the end of November sparked a run of four straight wins. The Seasiders were beaten by goals from a superb diving header by Barry Lloyd (on the ground in the picture above), and from Jimmy Conway. Cardiff were the next victims at the Cottage in an exciting 4-3 victory, the pick of the goals being the third by Steve Earle after he got on the end of a Conway cross.

This is a rare sight—Les Barrett heading a goal—but it was worth a point in a 2-2 draw at home to Middlesbrough just before Christmas. The first victory of 1972 was against Luton at the Cottage towards the end of January. George Johnston got two in the 3-1 win, but amazingly this was not one of them.

1971-72
DIVISION TWO

Fulham won only once during an eight-week spell around February—a 2-1 defeat of Bristol City at the Cottage. In the match, which marked goalkeeper Peter Mellor's Fulham debut, victory was sealed in style with a superb run and shot by Earle (two pictures above). But on the whole, the ball was not running Fulham's way at this time, as Roger Cross could testify. His header was brilliantly saved by the goalkeeper in the match which Cardiff won 1-0 at Ninian Park in March.

When Alan Mullery returned to the Cottage on loan, priceless points were
collected. Barry Lloyd's shot secured a draw at Burnley at the end of March.
Days later, Sheffield Wednesday were beaten 4-0 at the Cottage, only the
third win since the turn of the year. Mullers got the second that evening
from a penalty, after he himself had been fouled.

MATCH OF THE SEASON
Charlton 2 Fulham 2
8th April 1972

The hard-won promotion of the previous season was almost squandered immediately with some erratic and unconvincing performances, particularly after the turn of

the year. The controversial loan signing of Alan Mullery helped pick up vital points, but when Fulham travelled to the Valley, Mullery was back at Spurs, and it was an 'us or them' relegation clash.

All was set fair for the Cottagers when Steve Earle put them ahead (above), but they failed to capitalise on this early

advantage. Despite Fulham hitting the post and the bar, it was Charlton who scored next through Peter Hunt. In the second half the Robins went 2-1 up through Paul Went, but Fred Callaghan retrieved a priceless point for the Cottagers with a header (below). At the season's end three weeks later, it proved the decisive goal and point.

DIVISION TWO 1971-72 Final League Table

		P	W	D	L	F	A	Pts
1	Norwich	42	21	15	6	60	36	57
2	Birmingham	42	19	18	5	60	31	56
3	Millwall	42	19	17	6	64	46	55
4	QPR	42	20	14	8	57	28	54
5	Sunderland	42	17	19	9	67	57	50
6	Blackpool	42	20	7	15	70	50	47
7	Burnley	42	20	6	16	70	55	46
8	Bristol City	42	18	10	14	61	49	46
9	Middlesbrough	42	19	8	15	50	48	46
10	Carlisle	42	17	9	16	61	57	43
11	Swindon	42	15	12	15	47	47	42
12	Hull	42	14	10	18	49	53	38
13	Luton	42	10	18	14	43	48	38
14	Sheff Wed	42	13	12	17	51	58	38
15	Oxford	42	12	14	16	43	55	38
16	Portsmouth	42	12	13	17	59	68	37
17	Orient	42	14	9	19	50	61	37
18	Preston	42	12	12	18	52	58	36
19	Cardiff	42	10	14	18	56	69	34
20	**Fulham**	42	12	10	20	45	68	34
21	Charlton	42	12	9	21	55	77	33
22	Watford	42	5	9	28	24	75	19

SEASON 1972-73

DIVISION TWO

Alec Stock, one of football's most experienced managers, became Fulham's new boss. He replaced the outgoing Bill Dodgin, sacked just days after the 1971-72 season had ended. A man with a remarkable record at smaller clubs, Stock wasted no time in implementing his plans for the team and made two major early-season signings. Fulham paid a club record fee of £80,000 to bring defender Paul Went from Charlton, and £65,000 on old boy Alan Mullery from Spurs. Another

Back: John Cutbush, Fred Callaghan, Jimmy Dunne, Les Barrett, Steve Earle; front: Bill Taylor (coach), Barry Lloyd, Alan Mullery, Peter Mellor, John Mitchell, Paul Went, Ron Woolnough (physio), Jimmy Conway.

signing from Spurs was John Cutbush, a highly rated full-back. The team understandably took time to settle and it was not until October that both form and results began to improve. Newly promoted Aston Villa, who had also spent heavily, were beaten 2-0 at the Cottage before the season's best gate of 17,576.

Although the next couple of games were lost, the signs looked encouraging. A 3-1 reverse to Cardiff City in November was the only defeat in a 14-game run that yielded 20 points and pushed the Cottagers into a promotion challenging position. The run included two 5-1 home victories, against Brighton and Bristol City, and a creditable 2-2 draw away to top of the table Burnley. Two youngsters, winger Les Strong and centre-

forward John Mitchell, were drafted in from the reserves and both contributed in the belated promotion push. Mitchell, in his first season as a professional, finished with 11 goals, just four behind his striking partner and top scorer Steve Earle. A 2-1 defeat away to Nottingham Forest in the last week of February signalled the end of any realistic chance of promotion. The final placing of ninth would have been higher had it not been for the season's worst run of results; of the last ten games, six were lost, and only eight goals were scored.

A new season, a new manager (Alec Stock, right), and a
new captain (Alan Mullery), but it was still the same old
story. Too little firepower led to erratic results. Fulham
might have snatched a last-minute win in their opening
home game had John Richardson got on the end of a
cross (above). The following week at Middlesbrough,
Roger Cross put the Cottagers on the way to their first
away win with what was to prove his last goal for the
club.

F^FC
1972-73
DIVISION TWO

There was a satisfying 2-0 home win over Aston Villa in
October, with John Mitchell scoring the second, his first
goal at the Cottage (top opposite). The other picture
shows a crunch during the home match against Preston.
Dave Moreline seems to have come out tops.

FFC
1972-73
DIVISION TWO

Away games in the autumn yielded very little. A 1-2 defeat at Carlisle might have been a draw had John Cutbush put this chance away (left). At Hull, two John Mitchell goals earned a draw; his first is pictured centre opposite. Alan Mullery's header at the Manor Ground (below left) was the closest either Oxford or Fulham came to scoring.

Fulham won four of their first five games in 1973. The old firm of Earle and Barrett were in great form. Les scored the second in the 3-1 home win over Forest, then Steve got the second at Preston—another 3-1 victory—and the only goal of the game at home to Sheffield Wednesday.

MATCH OF THE SEASON
Fulham 5 Brighton 1
27th January 1973

In a rather ordinary mid-table season, Fulham occasionally showed flashes of class which, if sustained, would have brought promotion. The Cottagers' best performance that campaign, which lifted them into their highest position, fourth, was at home to bottom of the table Brighton.

With on-loan Alan Pinkney making his home debut and full-back John Fraser being given his third first-team outing, Fulham took the game to the visitors from the start. Steve Earle, with goal number 101, and John Mitchell, with his ninth in his first season, were on the mark in the first half. John Mitchell's goal is pictured at the top of the page. Bert Murray replied for the visitors, but after the break the reliable strike force of Earle, Conway and Barrett completed the rout. Steve Earle's goal, shown above, came courtesy of a typical Les Barrett run and pass; in the picture, Earle is on the edge of the goal area. Conway's goal (left) was a fierce shot from just inside the penalty area.

The win raised hopes of a serious promotion challenge. It was, however, the season's high-water mark, and a mere four wins in the last 15 games saw the club slide to ninth position in the table.

Fulham recorded only two away wins between the end of January and the end of the season. One of these was at Villa Park in March where John Mitchell scored once (right) in a fine 3-2 victory. Trips to Huddersfield and Blackpool yielded neither points nor goals but plenty of action for defenders Jimmy Dunne (above) and Paul Went (below).

The season rather petered out, but the name Conway appeared on the scoresheet in a creditable win at Portsmouth in April. This time it was John, who got both in a 2-1 success, the first (top) from a header. The last goals of the season were scored at Brisbane Road, where Fulham lost 2-3. Les Barrett got the first (above) from a very acute angle.

DIVISION TWO 1972-73 Final League Table

		P	W	D	L	F	A	Pts
1	Burnley	42	24	14	4	72	35	62
2	QPR	42	24	13	5	81	37	61
3	Aston Villa	42	18	14	10	51	47	50
4	Middlesbrough	42	17	13	12	46	43	47
5	Bristol City	42	17	12	13	63	51	46
6	Sunderland	42	17	12	13	59	49	46
7	Blackpool	42	18	10	14	56	51	46
8	Oxford	42	19	7	16	52	43	45
9	**Fulham**	**42**	**16**	**12**	**14**	**58**	**49**	**44**
10	Sheff Wed	42	17	10	15	59	55	44
11	Millwall	42	16	10	16	55	47	42
12	Luton	42	15	11	16	44	53	41
13	Hull	42	14	12	16	64	59	40
14	Nottm Forest	42	14	12	16	47	52	40
15	Orient	42	12	12	18	49	53	36
16	Swindon	42	10	16	16	46	60	36
17	Portsmouth	42	12	11	19	42	59	35
18	Carlisle	42	11	12	19	50	52	34
19	Preston	42	11	12	19	37	64	34
20	Cardiff	42	11	11	20	43	58	33
21	Huddersfield	42	8	17	17	36	56	33
22	Brighton	42	8	13	21	46	83	29

SEASON 1973-74

DIVISION TWO

At the start of the season, manager Alec Stock signed two players from his old club, Luton Town—Alan Slough, an experienced utility player, and Viv Busby, a forward that Stock had himself discovered while in charge at Kenilworth Road. Their combined fee of £70,000 underlined Fulham's and the manager's resolve to mount a serious promotion assault and restore First Division football. It took the club's spending to over £200,000 in just a year, and the investment looked like paying off.

Fulham got off to a flying start, heading the table after the first few games. For all the fans' optimism, however, the promotion challenge was not sustained. The root of the problem was goalscoring. Incredibly, Fulham failed to score in half of their 42 League games, averaging less than a goal a game. With the financial burden of the Riverside Stand coupled with a decline in attendances, Fulham were forced to sell two of their key players. Steve Earle, the club's top scorer in the previous three seasons, went to Leicester for £80,000, while Paul Went was sold to Portsmouth for £155,000. John Lacy took over the centre-half position and proved to be a more than adequate replacement for Went.

Ironically, Fulham's reshuffled side improved their results immediately. A good performance came in the F.A. Cup against First Division Leicester City. Although Fulham lost the fourth round tie 2-1 in a replay at Filbert Street, the highlight was a spectacular goal from Alan Mullery in the first game at the Cottage; it was voted the BBC Goal of the Season.

The remaining part of the season was spent in and around mid-table. Results fluctuated wildly. This was

Back row: Steve Scrivens, John Fraser, Les Strong, Dave Carlton, Trevor Porter, Tony Field, John Conway, Paul Shrubb, John O'Callaghan, Terry Bullivant; centre: John Collins (coach), Ron Woolnough (physio), Dave Moreline, Paul Went, John Dowie, John Lacy, Peter Mellor, Malcolm Webster, Viv Busby, John Mitchell, Ken Gladwin, John Cutbush, Bill Taylor (coach), Alec Stock (manager); front: Alan Slough, Jimmy Dunne, Fred Callaghan, Steve Earle, Chappie D'Amato (director), Alan Mullery, Les Barrett, Barry Lloyd, Jimmy Conway.

typified when the Cottagers lost three games either side of a winning four-match run. One crumb of comfort for the fans was the signing of Bobby Moore just prior to the transfer deadline. The West Ham and ex-England captain chose Fulham ahead of a number of clubs eager to sign him. Over 18,000 saw him make his debut at home against Jack Charlton's Middlesbrough, but the 4-0 scoreline went in favour of the soon to be crowned Second Division champions. Although Moore had reached the 'veteran' stage, the football world was destined to hear a lot of him next season.

It was the Conway-Earle-Barrett combination that gave Fulham a winning start to the 1973-74 campaign. Barrett got the first goal of the season (left) against Millwall at the Cottage (and Conway the second) in a 2-0 win. At Ayresome Park the following week, there was a similar scoreline, but this time Barrett and Earle were the marksmen (pictures below).

Peter Mellor made 66 consecutive appearances for Fulham after signing from Burnley in February 1972. Brave and acrobatic, his dynamic displays made him popular with supporters. Here he dives to head the ball away in the match at home to Bolton.

The last of Steve Earle's 98 League goals for Fulham before his move to Leicester was in a 1-2 defeat at Notts County in October.

F
F
C
1973-74
DIVISION TWO

Fulham scored a splendid 'double' over Sheffield Wednesday. In the 3-0 win at Hillsborough in December, John Conway and Viv Busby got the first and third goals (above and below).

Opposite page: New striker Viv Busby settled in quickly and scored some impressive goals. In the 3-1 home win over Oxford just before Christmas, he found the net twice; his second is pictured at top.

John Conway was enjoying an extended run in the first team until he was injured in the 0-1 defeat by Cardiff at the Cottage in the opening game of the New Year.

This is a rather static picture of an historic moment—the kick-off in the first-ever League match on a Sunday, set in motion by Alan Slough, on January 20th. The three-day week had led to restrictions on floodlights, and Millwall had put the game back to Sunday morning; the Lions won 1-0.

133

MATCH OF THE SEASON
Fulham 4   Sheffield Wednesday 1
2nd February 1974

The one bright spot in an otherwise mediocre season was the 'double' achieved over Sheffield Wednesday. A convincing 3-0 win at Hillsborough in December, the best away result of the campaign, was followed up by this impressive victory in the return six weeks later, which equalled the season's best home scoreline.

Viv Busby, a close-season signing from Luton, was the star of the show. With two goals in the first half and a third in the second, he notched his first ever hat-trick in League football. It was also the first in the League by a Fulham player since Steve Earle's treble at Stockport in September 1969, and the first by a Fulham player in the Second Division for almost 15 years, when Haynes got three against Rotherham in April 1959. Coincidentally, two other Fulham players have also scored hat-tricks against Wednesday in the period covered by this book—Jimmy Hill on Good Friday 1959, and Maurice Cook in September 1962, the first match at the Cottage under floodlights.

Viv Busby's second and third goals are shown in the pictures opposite.

Les Barrett completed the scoring for Fulham, whilst Wednesday's lone strike came in the first half from defender Danny Cameron. These were only a sideshow, however, for the day—and the match ball—belonged to Busby.

136

By beating Luton 2-1 at home in March, Fulham made it four wins on the trot. The second of Barry Lloyd's two goals was scored from a Les Barrett cross; Barry is on the ground in the picture left.

This was followed by three defeats, but when Forest visited the Cottage near the end of March, Fulham returned to winning ways. Jimmy Conway sealed the 2-0 victory when he finished off yet another Barrett cross.

At the end of March former England captain Alan Mullery volleyed a marvellous goal at Bristol City (above) to give Fulham a 1-0 win.

The signing of Bobby Moore had generated a lot of late-season excitement at the Cottage. Although Fulham lost 1-3 at home to Crystal Palace on Good Friday morning, this other former England captain got his first (and only) goal for his new club, with a magnificent volley.

Fulham got revenge for the Good Friday defeat by Palace, winning the return at Selhurst the following Tuesday by two goals to nil. Busby and Barrett were on target for the visitors. The defeat virtually condemned Palace to relegation for the second successive season.

		P	W	D	L	F	A	Pts
1	Middlesbrough	42	27	11	4	77	30	65
2	Luton	42	19	12	11	64	51	50
3	Carlisle	42	20	9	13	61	48	49
4	Orient	42	15	18	9	55	42	48
5	Blackpool	42	17	13	12	57	40	47
6	Sunderland	42	19	9	14	58	44	47
7	Nottm Forest	42	15	15	12	57	43	45
8	West Brom	42	14	16	12	48	45	44
9	Hull	42	13	17	12	46	47	43
10	Notts County	42	15	13	14	55	60	43
11	Bolton	42	15	12	15	44	40	42
12	Millwall	42	14	14	14	51	51	42
13	**Fulham**	**42**	**16**	**10**	**16**	**39**	**43**	**42**
14	Aston Villa	42	13	15	14	48	45	41
15	Portsmouth	42	14	12	16	45	62	40
16	Bristol City	42	14	10	18	47	54	38
17	Cardiff	42	10	16	16	49	62	36
18	Oxford	42	10	16	16	35	46	36
19	Sheff Wed	42	12	11	19	51	63	35
20	Crystal Palace	42	11	12	19	43	56	34
21	Preston*	42	9	14	19	40	62	31
22	Swindon	42	7	11	24	36	72	25

DIVISION TWO 1973-74 Final League Table

*Preston had one point deducted for fielding an ineligible player.

SEASON 1974-75

DIVISION TWO

Fulham started the season in tremendous style. After four games they led the table, having dropped just one point, and scoring nine goals in the process. Viv Busby in particular was in fine form, scoring four times. One of these was a brilliant effort. It came against Cardiff when he left the City defence in tatters with a run that started on the half-way line, before scoring one of the best goals ever seen at the Cottage.

With Bobby Moore and Alan Mullery both in outstanding form, it looked as though it could finally be Fulham's year. But the signs seemed all too familiar when Fulham failed to score in the next three games. And it was this lack of goals, especially from the recognised strikers, that became the pattern for the season. Indeed, in a 13-game run, just six goals were scored; three came from mid-fielder Alan Mullery, one from full-back John Cutbush, one from mid-fielder John Dowie, while the only Fulham forward to find the back of the net was Rod Belfitt, on loan from Sunderland.

The defence were having a much better season. Marshalled superbly by Bobby Moore, the defensive line-up remained largely unchanged. Goalkeeper Peter Mellor, Les Strong and centre-half John Lacy missed just a handful of games between them throughout the season.

Undoubtedly, the greater glories came in the two major cup competitions. In the Football League Cup, Fulham enjoyed a good run, knocking out holders Wolves at Molineux 3-1 and West Ham 2-1, before going down 0-3 away to Newcastle. But in the F.A. Cup Fulham did even better. After taking seven games to get to the fifth round, the Cottagers then swept all before

Back row: Steve Scrivens, Ken Gladwin, Michael Kerslake, Tyrone James, Ernie Howe, Paul Sargent, Trevor Porter, Dave Collier, John Byatt, Flemming Hansen, Tony Field, Brian Greenaway, Paul Shrubb, Nick Sparks; centre: Alec Stock (manager), Bill Taylor (coach), Jimmy Dunne, John Mitchell, Joe Peck, John Lacy, Peter Mellor, Alan Slough, Peter Feeley, Viv Busby, John Dowie, Ron Woolnough (physio), John Collins (coach); front: Terry Bullivant, John Fraser, John Conway, Les Barrett, Jimmy Conway, Alan Mullery, Bobby Moore, John Cutbush, Barry Lloyd, Les Strong, Barry Friend.

them. Playing adventurous and attacking football, they disposed of three First Division sides on the way to the club's first-ever appearance in the F.A. Cup Final.

The progress in the Cup coincided with an upturn in League form. Fulham went to second place Sunderland and inflicted on them their first home defeat of the season. It came as a welcome win, with Fulham just a couple of points from the bottom places. It was the start of a nine-match sequence that produced six wins and a healthy mid-table position.

Alan Mullery was voted Footballer of the Year, the first Fulham player to receive the accolade. Although the Cup final was eventually lost, it proved to be a fitting climax to a very exciting season.

MATCH OF THE SEASON
Fulham 1 Manchester United 2
5th October 1974

In a season dominated by Cup football, it is easy to overlook the fact there was some exciting League action on offer. Appropriately, on the weekend which marked the anniversary of the record crowd at the Cottage, a season's best gate of 26,513 turned out for the visit of Tommy Docherty's exciting young Manchester United side. The Red Devils led the Second Division and Fulham were fifth, and the game was selected by the BBC for Match of the Day.

The match lived up to expectations, although there was general agreement that a draw would have been a fairer reflection of the play. Typical of Fulham's efforts was a fine first-half shot from Jimmy Conway, shown above. United's two goals, one in each half, came from Stuart Pearson, whilst Fulham's goal was a second-half effort by Viv Busby (left). The visitors had Alex Stepney to thank for holding on to both points. The goalkeeper made two outstanding saves late in the game, and by the final whistle, it was the United fans who were calling for time.

Although Viv Busby is best remembered for his Cup heroics in 1974-75, he gave notice with a couple of specials early in the League campaign—a remarkable goal in the 4-0 win in the first home match, against Cardiff (top opposite), and another (left) when Norwich were beaten by a similar scoreline at the Cottage in September. In between, Notts County had been beaten 3-0, and Busby's former Luton colleague, Alan Slough, showed he, too, was capable of a spectacular strike; this header opened the scoring.

The crowd share the players' joy after a long-range shot from Alan Mullery (No. 4, top left picture) had flown into the net for a 1-0 home victory over Blackpool in November.

Left: On-loan striker Rod Belfitt from Sunderland saved a point with a goal at Nottingham Forest.

Bottom left: Here's another match-winning strike from Alan Mullery, this time in the home match against West Brom in December. Bobby Moore tapped a free-kick to him and he smashed the ball past an incredulous wall.

This page: The Cup run helped to lift the League form, and Sheffield Wednesday and Southampton were both beaten at the Cottage. Les Barrett got the first against Wednesday in the 2-1 win, and the winner in a five-goal thriller against the Saints.

Out for much of the season with injury, John Mitchell staked his claim for a Cup semi-final place with a goal at Bristol Rovers in March. It was the winner and Mitch's first goal of the season.

Just three days after the glory night at Maine Road, Fulham were back in Manchester, at Old Trafford. The Second Division champions-elect won 1-0, but a bubbling John Mitchell kept them on their toes (top). His run of good form continued with both goals in the 2-2 home draw against Portsmouth, the second (above) a marvellous header from a Barrett cross.

		P	W	D	L	F	A	Pts
1	Man United	42	26	9	7	66	30	61
2	Aston Villa	42	25	8	9	69	32	58
3	Norwich	42	20	13	9	58	37	53
4	Sunderland	42	19	13	10	65	35	51
5	Bristol City	42	21	8	13	47	33	50
6	West Brom	42	18	9	15	54	42	45
7	Blackpool	42	14	17	11	38	33	45
8	Hull	42	15	14	13	40	53	44
9	**Fulham**	**42**	**13**	**16**	**13**	**44**	**39**	**42**
10	Bolton	42	15	12	15	45	41	42
11	Oxford	42	15	12	15	41	51	42
12	Orient	42	11	20	11	28	39	42
13	Southampton	42	15	11	16	53	54	41
14	Notts County	42	12	16	14	49	59	40
15	York	42	14	10	18	51	55	38
16	Nottm Forest	42	12	14	16	43	55	38
17	Portsmouth	42	12	13	17	44	54	37
18	Oldham	42	10	15	17	40	48	35
19	Bristol Rovers	42	12	11	19	42	64	35
20	Millwall	42	10	12	20	44	56	32
21	Cardiff	42	9	14	19	36	62	32
22	Sheff Wed	42	5	11	26	29	64	21

DIVISION TWO 1974-75 Final League Table

SEASON 1975-76

DIVISION TWO

With the same squad that had reached Wembley the previous May, Fulham began the new season amongst the early promotion favourites. In the opening matches, they lived up to their billing, finishing September in third place. Particularly impressive were victories over West Brom and Chelsea at the Cottage and a rare win against Oxford at the Manor Ground. The 15 goals scored in the first nine matches were shared between six players, with central defender Ernie Howe

proving not only a capable deputy for the injured Lacy at the back, but also a potent threat up front with four goals.

When the goals dried up in the autumn, the Cottagers started to slide down the table. In 14 games from the start of October to the turn of the year, they managed to score more than one goal in a match on only three occasions. By taking just 13 points from these fixtures, they dropped to mid-table, and the season virtually ended when Huddersfield won in the third round of the Cup at the Cottage in the first match in 1976.

Over the rest of the League programme, Fulham averaged less than a point a game, 15 points from 19 matches, and finished a disappointing 12th. With just two wins in the final 13 games, and a mere six goals, they had to be grateful for having enough points in the bag not to have to worry about relegation.

Back row: Paul Howes, Gary Palmer, Tyrone James, John Dowie, John Margerrison, Steven Hatter, Dennis Byatt, Michael Kerslake, Brian Greenaway, Terry Bullivant, Steve Scrivens; standing: Ted Drake (assistant manager), Les Barrett, Barry Lloyd, Viv Busby, John Lacy, Paul Sargent, Peter Mellor, Trevor Porter, Ernie Howe, Steve Camp, Alan Slough, John Mitchell, John Fraser, John Cutbush, Ron Woolnough (physio); seated: Graham Hortop (secretary), Les Strong, Bill Taylor (coach), Bobby Moore, Alan Mullery, Jimmy Conway, Terry Medwin (coach), Barry Friend, Alec Stock (manager).

The season ended on a sad note with the departure of Alan Mullery after 412 matches stretching back to 1959. His only substitute appearance was in his final game, a 1-3 defeat at West Brom. Relations with the club were strained at the end when the expected coaching job did not materialise, and he chose his appearance on 'This Is Your Life' to announce his retirement.

The Cup final raised League expectations in August, and Fulham started well enough. Carlisle, quarter-final opponents the previous March, were brushed aside 3-0 at the Cottage, two of the goals coming from Viv Busby and Alan Slough. Days later, Fulham returned from a trip to Bolton with a point, Busby scoring the first in a 2-2 draw.

MATCH OF THE SEASON
Fulham 4 West Brom 0
30th August 1975

After the Cup success of the previous season, Fulham began 1975-76 amongst the promotion favourites, and their early season form confirmed their status. The visit of West Brom was the BBC's choice for Match of the Day, a decision which proved to be well justified.

Attention was focussed on reserve central defender Ernie Howe, deputising for the injured John Lacy. He had the task of marking Albion's new striker, Geoff Hurst. Not only did Howe blot out the former England star completely, but he also found time to go upfield and score two spectacular goals, both headers. He scored his first just before half-time; his second, shown above, was a magnificent diving effort in the 57th minute. Either side of these two were two more headed goals—from John Mitchell and Viv Busby (pictured below).

This was a totally convincing victory which lifted Fulham into third place in the table. Sadly, they failed to maintain this sparkling form, and in the end had to settle for 12th place.

In September, Fulham recorded some fine victories, and opposite are three of the goals they scored. Jimmy Conway got one of the two which beat Chelsea at the Cottage; Busby scored a splendid goal in an impressive 3-1 win at Oxford; and at Hull, Barry Lloyd got the winner in a 2-1 success.

^FF_C
1975-76
DIVISION TWO

Points started to slip away in October. Despite Ernie Howe's fifth goal of the season at home to Orient (above), the match was drawn. Jimmy Conway's double at home to Luton in November put an end to the rot, bringing Fulham's first home win for two months. Jimmy's first goal that day is shown below.

December 1975 was a memorable month for headed goals (pictures on this page). Ernie Howe was on the mark in a 2-2 draw at Oldham; this was his sixth goal, making him the season's top scorer at that stage. Alan Slough's powerful header was the best goal of the three in the match against Bolton, but the visitors took the points. Boxing Day saw Notts County at the Cottage. John Mitchell enjoyed himself with two in his side's 3-2 win; this was his first goal.

F^FC
1975-76
DIVISION TWO

Opposite page, top: A dramatic photo of a great goal, scored by Alan Slough to clinch the 2-0 win over York in February. Right: The same month saw a similar scoreline against Sunderland; both goals were scored by Viv Busby, and his first is shown in the picture.

By scoring against Hull at the Cottage in April (above), John Mitchell reached double figures for the first time. He was top scorer and, with ever-present Peter Mellor, was one of the successes of a mediocre season (top pictures).

		P	W	D	L	F	A	Pts
	DIVISION TWO 1975-76 Final League Table							
1	Sunderland	42	24	8	10	67	36	56
2	Bristol City	42	19	15	8	59	35	53
3	West Brom	42	20	13	9	50	33	53
4	Bolton	42	20	12	10	64	38	52
5	Notts County	42	19	11	12	60	41	49
6	Southampton	42	21	7	14	66	50	49
7	Luton	42	19	10	13	61	51	48
8	Nottm Forest	42	17	12	13	55	40	46
9	Charlton	42	15	12	15	61	72	42
10	Blackpool	42	14	14	14	40	49	42
11	Chelsea	42	12	16	14	53	54	40
12	**Fulham**	**42**	**13**	**14**	**15**	**45**	**47**	**40**
13	Orient	42	13	14	15	37	39	40
14	Hull	42	14	11	17	45	49	39
15	Blackburn	42	12	14	16	45	50	38
16	Plymouth	42	13	12	17	48	54	38
17	Oldham	42	13	12	17	57	68	38
18	Bristol Rovers	42	11	16	15	38	50	38
19	Carlisle	42	12	13	17	45	59	37
20	Oxford	42	11	11	20	39	59	33
21	York	42	10	8	24	39	71	28
22	Portsmouth	42	9	7	26	32	61	25

SEASON 1976-77

DIVISION TWO

This was a season that saw dramatic changes both on and off the pitch. The appointment of new director Ernie Clay signalled the start of many comings and goings that continued throughout the campaign. England team coach Bill Taylor left for Manchester City along with Jimmy Conway. Bobby Campbell arrived from Arsenal to replace Taylor and, within months, was to take over from manager Alec Stock. In the boardroom, Tommy Trinder stood down as chairman and, after many years at the Cottage, club secretary Graham Hortop left.

The turnover on the playing side was just as high, with ten new players arriving at the Cottage in the course of the season. The first of these were George Best and Rodney Marsh, a headline-making duo who attracted over 21,000 to the Cottage to watch their first game, against Bristol Rovers. Best needed just two touches and 71 seconds to score the game's only goal. Millions watched weeks later on television when both put on another super show in a 4-1 victory over Hereford. But these performances were not sustained. The next game resulted in a heavy 4-1 defeat by bottom club Southampton that also saw George Best sent off.

Results deteriorated dramatically and just three victories came from the next 24 League games. It was during this period that the first murmurings of discontent were heard against new manager Bobby Campbell who was never fully accepted by the Fulham fans. He was, however, a shrewd operator in the transfer market, bringing some very good players to the Cottage. These included goalkeeper Gerry Peyton from

Back row: Steve Scrivens, Tyrone James, Les Strong, Rodney Marsh, Viv Busby, John Mitchell, Terry Bullivant; centre: Barry Lloyd, John Evanson, Ernie Howe, Peter Mellor, Richard Teale, John Lacy, John Dowie, Bobby Moore, Alec Stock (manager); front: Ken Craggs (coach), Les Barrett, George Best, Bobby Campbell (assistant manager), Alan Slough, John Cutbush, Ron Woolnough (physio).

Burnley, Chelsea forward Teddy Maybank and experienced full-back Ray Evans from Millwall, bought to replace John Cutbush who left to join Sheffield United.

Relegation came uncomfortably close and was only avoided by a late run that brought 14 points from the last dozen games. Included in this run was a fine 3-1 triumph over top of the table Chelsea, the goals coming from George Best, John Mitchell and recent signing Alan Warboys. But many supporters remember the game for a wild Peter Storey 'tackle' on Ray Lewington, a young Chelsea mid-field player who one day would become both a Fulham player and a Fulham manager.

The Cottage faithful were treated to something a bit special in August and September 1976. Les Barrett's fine goal earned a point in the opening game against Nottingham Forest, whilst by the time of the second match, both George Best and Rodney Marsh, pictured in the Charlton dug-out, were in the side. (Even photographers are human enough to want star autographs.) George Best marked his debut with a first-minute winner against Bristol Rovers (left), as he and Rodney Marsh, back at Fulham after ten years, created an air of expectancy.

F F C
1976-77
DIVISION TWO

Marsh lost no time getting his name on the scoresheet, and this classic strike at Luton (right), the second goal in a 2-0 win, had the stamp of quality all over it. The big-name personalities tended to obscure the consistent displays of players like John Lacy, a tower of strength at the heart of the defence. The picture above right shows him supporting the attack in the match against Cardiff.

John Mitchell revelled in the improved service supplied by Best and Marsh. He was on the mark with his head at Plymouth in November, and scored twice in a thrilling 5-0 home win over Oldham a month later (left). In between, he took over as goalkeeper against Notts County when Peter Mellor was stretchered off, and Fulham lost 1-5. By the time Blackburn visited West London just before Christmas, the club was going through behind-the-scenes traumas, which resulted in Alec Stock's departure. The players were not disturbed, however, and Best's goal (below) was the second in a 2-0 win.

F^FC
1976-77
DIVISION TWO

Bobby Campbell became Fulham's new manager, and it was 13 games before Fulham won. The biggest crowd to see Fulham play that season (55,003) was at Stamford Bridge, where Howe showed stylish action (above), but it was a goalless and pointless journey for the Cottagers. At least they scored against Bristol Rovers at Eastville in February through a John Mitchell goal (below), but they still lost; whilst Hereford's goalkeeper Hughes (right) had to take unusual measures, but still ended up on the winning side.

One of manager Bobby Campbell's first signings was Alan Warboys, who
scored on his home debut, in the 1-2 defeat by Luton.

Fulham's first home success since before Christmas finally came at the
end of March with a 3-2 win over Sheffield United. For his second, and
Fulham's third, goal that day (below), Teddy Maybank pounced on a
rebound and superbly hit the ball first time into goal from a narrow angle.

MATCH OF THE SEASON
Fulham 3 Chelsea 1
8th April 1977

A season of turmoil reached its climax on Good Friday when Chelsea visited the Cottage. The largest crowd of the season (29,690) came to see relegation-threatened Fulham play their neighbours from the Bridge, who were looking odds on for promotion. The Cottagers had achieved just two victories in the 15 matches they had played since Bobby Campbell had replaced Alec Stock as manager, and they were in desperate need of a win. On the day they were good value for the points.

The home side attacked Chelsea from the start, and outplayed and outfought the Division's leaders for the whole 90 minutes. The first goal came after 11 minutes from Alan Warboys, a recent signing from Bristol Rovers, who dived to head home from John Mitchell. Just nine minutes later it was 2-0, when George Best fired in following Bonetti's poor punch out (right). Two minutes after the interval, Mitchell made the game safe (below); he swept the ball into goal following a move that also involved Warboys and Teddy Maybank. Ray Wilkins' 77th-minute goal for the Blues was no more than a consolation.

This win, marred only by Peter Storey's fourth booking in six games for Fulham, virtually assured the Cottagers of Second Division survival, but defeat did not stop Chelsea progressing to Division One.

At least Fulham's home programme ended on a high note. Orient were thrashed 6-1, with John Mitchell scoring a personal best four goals, including the powerful header pictured at the top. It was also Bobby Moore's final game in London, before he retired after the visit to Blackburn the following week.

		P	W	D	L	F	A	Pts
1	Wolves	42	22	13	7	84	45	57
2	Chelsea	42	21	13	8	73	53	55
3	Nottm Forest	42	21	10	11	77	43	52
4	Bolton	42	20	11	11	74	54	51
5	Blackpool	42	17	17	8	58	42	51
6	Luton	42	23	6	15	67	48	48
7	Charlton	42	16	16	10	71	58	48
8	Notts County	42	19	10	13	65	60	48
9	Southampton	42	17	10	15	72	67	44
10	Millwall	42	17	13	14	57	53	43
11	Sheff United	42	14	12	16	54	63	40
12	Blackburn	42	15	9	18	42	54	39
13	Oldham	42	14	10	18	52	64	38
14	Hull	42	10	17	15	45	53	37
15	Bristol Rovers	42	12	13	17	53	68	37
16	Burnley	42	11	14	17	46	64	36
17	**Fulham**	**42**	**11**	**13**	**18**	**44**	**61**	**35**
18	Cardiff	42	12	10	20	56	67	34
19	Orient	42	9	16	17	37	55	34
20	Carlisle	42	11	12	19	49	75	34
21	Plymouth	42	8	16	18	46	65	32
22	Hereford	42	8	15	19	57	78	31

DIVISION TWO 1976-77 Final League Table

SEASON 1977-78

DIVISION TWO

B ans, resignations and money demands were the unwelcome headlines that preceded the new season. With monies on fees still outstanding, Fulham were banned by the Football League from signing any new players. A board meeting in July resulted in five of the seven directors resigning. It was closely followed by a demand by the builders McAlpine for immediate payment for the Riverside Stand. Eliminated from the opening round of the League Cup by Orient, Fulham also started badly in the League. It was five games before they registered their first win, a 5-1 home victory over

Back: Michael Kerslake, John Evanson, John Margerrison, Dennis Byatt, John Mitchell, Tyrone James, Tony Mahoney; centre: Ken Craggs (coach), Steve Hatter, Tony Gale, Gerry Peyton, Ernie Howe, Perry Digweed, John Lacy, Ray Evans, Ron Woolnough (physio); front: Brian Greenaway, Terry Bullivant, Peter Storey, Bobby Campbell (manager), Les Strong, Teddy Maybank, Les Barrett.

Notts County. This was followed by a 3-2 away win over third-placed Crystal Palace and a 4-1 home victory against Burnley. The deteriorating financial position forced the club into parting with a number of established players. Peter Storey and Alan Warboys went after only a few weeks of the season and were quickly followed by George Best, who returned to America. Teddy Maybank went to Brighton for £200,000 while defender Ernie Howe joined QPR for £50,000. The departure of so many experienced players was cushioned by the availability of skilful home-grown youngsters such as

Tony Mahoney, Brian Greenaway, Terry Bullivant and the highly talented Tony Gale.

With the ban on transfers lifted, Fulham paid £50,000 for Scunthorpe defender Richard Money. He made his debut in one of Fulham's better performances when they

beat League leaders Bolton 2-0. That result was the start of an improved second half to the season which continued with seven wins and three draws from 12 games. A heavy defeat away to Blackburn, themselves in contention for promotion, brought the first defeat of the New Year and the end of any hopes Fulham had of joining the leaders. As in previous seasons, goalscoring was the major problem. A total of 49 League goals was scored, with John Mitchell's nine making him top scorer of the season. In the closing weeks, however, a new name made its debut on the scoring list. Gordon Davies got the winner at Blackpool, the first of the goals that would eventually take him past Johnny Haynes' club record.

Goals were hard to come by at the start of the season. Teddy Maybank was the most regular threat to opposing defences and was unlucky not to score at Bristol Rovers in August (above). A John Mitchell hat-trick in a 5-1 home win over Notts County in September finally ended the drought. In the picture below, John is seen scoring his hat-trick goal from 25 yards out.

Teenager Tony Gale made the breakthrough in 1977-78, and in October he scored his first-ever goal in a 3-2 win at Crystal Palace (top opposite). In the centre picture, a Burnley defender finds that even though George Best was 31 years old, there was only one sure way to stop him. The visit of Blackpool to the Cottage the same month yielded Fulham a point in a 1-1 draw. The Cottagers' goal came from Tony Mahoney (bottom opposite) with a remarkable headed goal from the edge of the penalty area.

$$F^F_C$$

1977-78
DIVISION TWO

MATCH OF THE SEASON
Fulham 3 Sunderland 3
5th November 1977

This was a good old-fashioned thriller, an autumnal Second Division encounter between two mid-table teams. The only source of regret was that a mere 10,548 turned up at the Cottage to see it. The absentees missed six goals scored by six different players, a performance from George Best which brought back memories of earlier glories and a dramatic finale that included a missed penalty and a last-gasp equaliser.

The goals were evenly distributed across the two periods. A close-range John Mitchell strike (below), and a shot by George Best from the edge of the box (bottom), put the home side on top, to which the Wearsiders responded with a goal by Roy Greenwood. After the break, the visitors took the lead through Gary Rowell and Kevin Arnott, but, with five minutes left, Fulham looked set for a share of the points when they were awarded a penalty—only for Teddy Maybank to miss from the spot (centre picture opposite). However, he redeemed himself with just 60 seconds to go, as shown in the subsequent picture, when he got his head to a swirling cross and steered the ball past Barry Siddall from close range. The explosive finish was an entirely appropriate way to celebrate Guy Fawkes Day. The football throughout was exciting and of a high standard; it hardly seemed necessary for Les Strong to show George Best just how it should be done (right).

Opposite page: Despite his youth, Tony Gale showed he could score equally well with either headers or shots. The top picture shows a headed goal—at home to Orient in October; Tony is third right. Fulham lost that match 1-2, but the following month beat Hull 2-0 at the Cottage, Tony scoring one of the goals with a fierce shot from 20 yards.

The week before the visit of Hull, George Best had played his last match for Fulham in the 0-2 defeat at Stoke (bottom picture).

F F
C

Brian Greenaway had a habit of popping up to score some vital goals. The shot shown above, however, hit a Millwall defender on its way in, and was deemed an own goal. It came in a 3-0 win at the Den in December. On Boxing Day, the Cottagers travelled to Mansfield, where John Mitchell scored (below), but the team lost 1-2.

Fulham's December signing from
Scunthorpe, Richard Money, made an
immediate impact at the Cottage. He
scored with a long-range shot in the
exciting 2-0 home win over Alan
Mullery's Brighton (top opposite). Brian
Greenaway showed his goal-poaching
instincts in January at Charlton, and in
February at home to Spurs, with the
winner and equaliser respectively.

F^FC

1977-78
DIVISION TWO

The headed goal by Tony Gale shown
above, deserved to win any match. It
was the only score in Fulham's home
game against Cardiff in March. John
Evanson was a tireless worker in
midfield, and he occasionally got forward
into scoring positions, as here against
Palace. He was denied this time, but did
score Fulham's goal in a 1-1 draw.

Both full-backs liked to get forward in 1977-78. Skipper Ray Evans scored four goals, and the top picture shows the fourth of them, the winner at Hull in April. Les Strong was less prolific, but he still had a go. Here he is denied by Eric Steele in the Brighton goal.

		P	W	D	L	F	A	Pts
DIVISION TWO 1977-78 Final League Table								
1	Bolton	42	24	10	8	63	33	58
2	Southampton	42	22	13	7	70	39	57
3	Tottenham	42	20	16	6	83	49	56
4	Brighton	42	22	12	8	63	38	56
5	Blackburn	42	16	13	13	56	60	45
6	Sunderland	42	14	16	12	67	59	44
7	Stoke	42	16	10	16	53	49	42
8	Oldham	42	13	16	13	54	58	42
9	Crystal Palace	42	13	15	14	50	47	41
10	**Fulham**	42	14	13	15	49	49	41
11	Burnley	42	15	10	17	56	64	40
12	Sheff United	42	16	8	18	62	73	40
13	Luton	42	14	10	18	54	52	38
14	Orient	42	10	18	14	43	49	38
15	Notts County	42	11	16	15	54	62	38
16	Millwall	42	12	14	16	49	57	38
17	Charlton	42	13	12	17	55	68	38
18	Bristol Rovers	42	13	12	17	61	77	38
19	Cardiff	42	13	12	17	51	71	38
20	Blackpool	42	12	13	17	59	60	37
21	Mansfield	42	10	11	21	49	69	31
22	Hull	42	8	12	22	34	52	28

SEASON 1978-79

DIVISION TWO

This was Fulham's most successful season under Bobby Campbell's aegis, but there was a feeling in May 1979 that more could have been achieved. A poor start—two League defeats and elimination from the League Cup by lowly Darlington—was followed by an impressive run that left the Cottagers needing to beat Blackburn at home in order to top the table in November. Predictably, they lost.

Standing: Ian Salter (youth team coach), Ron Woolnough (physio), Tony Mahoney, Steve Hatter, Tony Gale, Gerry Peyton, Perry Digweed, Geoff Banton, Kevin Lock, John Margerrison, Mike Kelly (coach); seated: Gordon Boyd, John Evanson, Terry Bullivant, Bobby Campbell (manager), Brian Greenaway, Richard Money, Les Strong, Gordon Davies.

The improvement in form coincided with two new signings, striker Chris Guthrie and midfielder John Beck. Guthrie finished the season as top scorer, and he helped a young Gordon Davies to find his feet in League football. In the 1-0 win at Crystal Palace in October Davies picked up an achilles injury from which he was to suffer for the next ten years. This was 'the game of three halves', where the referee, realising he had blown the final whistle too early, brought the teams back out for the last five minutes in a near-deserted Selhurst Park.

To strengthen the promotion push, Campbell bought Scottish winger Peter Marinello in December; then in February he bought Peter Kitchen, for whom he paid a club record fee. Although a proven goalscorer, Kitchen's form deserted him at Fulham. In the 17 games after his signing, the Cottagers won just twice, scoring only 15 goals in the process. This was hardly promotion form, and the pre-Christmas promise ended in mid-table blandness.

171

F^FC

FFC
1978-79
DIVISION TWO

In the early games, young John Margerrison made quite an impression in front of goal. He got the opening goal of the season in a 1-3 defeat at Bristol Rovers (top), and then won the game at West Ham with a finely judged lob. His partner up front at this time was Tony Mahoney, seen in the picture at right powering past a West Ham defender, watched by Geoff Banton.

A worrying lack of firepower forced manager Campbell into the transfer market, and he bought nomadic Chris Guthrie from Swindon. He opened his scoring account at Oldham in September 1978 (top), a match Fulham won 2-0. His partner Gordon Davies got the second (above). Guthrie's presence sparked the other players, including Brian Greenaway who got one of the goals in the 2-0 home win over Stoke in October.

MATCH OF THE SEASON
Fulham 5 Preston North End 3
21st October 1978

The only time during Bobby Campbell's reign that Fulham looked like promotion candidates was in the autumn of 1978. When Preston visited the Cottage, Fulham were in fifth place having won five and drawn one of their previous seven games. Strengthened by new signing John Beck making his home debut in midfield, the Cottagers turned on their best display of the season.

It took the home side just seven minutes to open the scoring, Gordon Davies fastening on to a Chris Guthrie knock-down. Alex Bruce and Mike Baxter took advantage of defensive lapses to put the visitors ahead, but just before half-time, Baxter scored for Fulham. Under pressure from Davies, he lobbed the ball over his own keeper.

Within 15 minutes of the re-start, the Cottagers had a two-goal advantage. First Richard Money struck the ball from 30 yards into the Preston net (above), and then Kevin Lock hammered home from 12 yards

out (top opposite). The goal of the game came in the 63rd minute when Guthrie ran through the Preston defence for Fulham's fifth (below right). The visitors reduced the arrears through Coleman in the 72nd minute, but the home side were still very much in control.

The match also remains in the memory for the incident pictured below. Preston manager Nobby Stiles became incensed at an official's decision, and appeared to want to remonstrate personally. He was restrained in no uncertain fashion by Bobby Campbell.

Opposite page: The strange game against Palace at Selhurst, when the referee had some difficulty keeping time, was settled by yet another opportunist strike by Brian Greenaway (top).

Fulham could have gone to the top of the table in November if they had beaten Blackburn at home. Despite Ray Evans' powerful free-kick goal (centre), they slipped up 1-2. A 3-0 win at a foggy Cottage over Bristol Rovers the next week helped to restore confidence. The bottom picture shows the first of Guthrie's two goals that evening.

F F C
1978-79
DIVISION TWO

Few Fulham strikers in living memory were as consistently effective in the air as Chris Guthrie. His goal at home to Newcastle in December 1978 (shown above) was one of the best, and took the edge off a 1-3 defeat. The same month, John Margerrison staked his claim for 'Goal of the Season' with an unstoppable shot against Cambridge (below), the second of five Fulham scored that day.

F^FC

FFC
1978-79
DIVISION TWO

Above: this was one 'own goal' that Gordon Davies did not claim. Luton's Mark Aizlewood beats his own goalkeeper, Jake Findlay, for the only goal of the game.

Chris Guthrie's aerial power was again much in evidence, as he soared to equalise against Sunderland at home in January (right), and at Preston in March.

In his first full season in the side, Gordon Davies reached a respectable double figure goal tally. His goal against Charlton at the Cottage in March (centre right) was as good as any he scored in his long Fulham career. Also on the mark in the 3-1 win was skipper Ray Evans with a typical long-range drive (top). Record signing Peter Kitchen never found his best form at the Cottage, but he got a few spectacular goals, like the header shown above, which earned a point at Wrexham. The other picture shows Fulham's goal from the 1-1 draw at Notts County. Chris Guthrie, once again, leaps high to beat the goalkeeper and head into the net.

In an attempt to enter the Guinness Book of Records for goalmouth packing, Fulham and Notts County players fell over themselves at Meadow Lane in April. Nothing came of their efforts, however. The match was drawn 1-1.

DIVISION TWO 1978-79 Final League Table

		P	W	D	L	F	A	Pts
1	Crystal Palace	42	19	19	4	51	24	57
2	Brighton	42	23	10	9	72	39	56
3	Stoke	42	20	16	6	58	31	56
4	Sunderland	42	22	11	9	70	44	55
5	West Ham	42	18	14	10	70	39	50
6	Notts County	42	14	16	12	48	60	44
7	Preston	42	12	18	12	59	57	42
8	Newcastle	42	17	8	17	51	55	42
9	Cardiff	42	16	10	16	56	70	42
10	**Fulham**	**42**	**13**	**15**	**14**	**50**	**47**	**41**
11	Orient	42	15	10	17	51	51	40
12	Cambridge	42	12	16	14	44	52	40
13	Burnley	42	14	12	16	51	62	40
14	Oldham	42	13	13	16	52	61	39
15	Wrexham	42	12	14	16	45	42	38
16	Bristol Rovers	42	14	10	18	48	60	38
17	Leicester	42	10	17	15	43	52	37
18	Luton	42	13	10	19	60	57	36
19	Charlton	42	11	13	18	60	69	35
20	Sheff United	42	11	12	19	52	69	34
21	Millwall	42	11	10	21	42	61	32
22	Blackburn	42	10	10	22	41	72	30

SEASON 1979-80

DIVISION TWO

Few seasons have opened with such a bang for Fulham but ended so miserably. A remarkable 4-3 win at Birmingham in the first match lifted the spirits, but a run of five straight defeats in September and October lowered supporters' expectations. By the end of the year, with just six wins in 22 games, even survival looked optimistic.

Manager Bobby Campbell started with basically the same squad as the previous season minus influential skipper Ray Evans, who went to Stoke, and without midfielders John Evanson and John

Margerrison. By the time he went into the transfer market to strengthen the squad, the Cottagers' fate was virtually sealed. There were nevertheless some valuable acquisitions. Sean O'Driscoll from Alvechurch, Roger Brown from Norwich and Ray Lewington from Wimbledon would all be influential figures at the club, but only after relegation had been confirmed and Campbell had departed.

A mini-revival, spurred by the loan signing of Howard Gayle and the return of Teddy Maybank, added some respectability to the season's record. However, too much ground had been lost in the first two-thirds of the season for Fulham to give themselves a

Back row: Terry Mancini (coach), John Beck, Tony Mahoney, Mike Kelly (coach), Tommy Mason, Gordon Davies, Ron Woolnough (physio); centre: Peter Kitchen, Kevin Lock, Gerry Peyton, Geoff Banton, Perry Digweed, Steve Hatter, Tony Gale, Mark Lovell; front: Peter Marinello, Brian Greenaway, Richard Money, Bobby Campbell (manager), Terry Bullivant, Les Strong, Chris Guthrie.

realistic chance of avoiding the drop. The team was by no means the worst Fulham side of the 1970s, but it found itself relegated at the end of the season because it lacked confidence and because its best players did not lead by example. In the end, the fight seemed to drain away from them.

MATCH OF THE SEASON
Birmingham City 3 Fulham 4
18th August 1979

The season opened with a bang. Not only did Fulham win away from home against a side that had just come down from Division One, but they did it the hard way, by giving the Blues a three-goal start. Any hopes, however, that this dramatic win might be the start of a long-awaited promotion push had evaporated by autumn, and the Cottagers finished the season in the relegation zone.

In the first half, Fulham were over-run by a Birmingham side inspired by new signing and captain Archie Gemmill, and Fulham's reserve keeper, Perry Digweed, was beaten three times in the opening 45 minutes. The second half saw a startling turnaround with Gordon Davies the hero. His header from a Tony Gale flick-on in the 52nd minute (above) started the comeback. Peter Marinello was creating havoc down the Blues left flank, and he set up goals two and three. For the second (left,

Chris Guthrie headed bravely in following Peter's cross, and for the third it was Gordon Davies who hurled himself at another pin-point Marinello pass. In the picture above, Les Strong, in the goalmouth, watches the ball cross the line. The storybook comeback was completed nine minutes from time, when Ivor rounded off his first hat-trick for Fulham (above right), thus sealing a famous victory, and ensuring he ended up with the match ball.

Left: Tony Gale steals upfield at Roker and heads a splendid equaliser, but Sunderland scored again to start a long series of odd-goal defeats for Fulham.

Gordon Davies was in lethal form in the opening month of the season, and he scored twice in Fulham's 3-1 home win over Burnley, the best goal of the day being this diving header, right. At the other end, Gerry Peyton was performing his customary restrained heroics in goal.

F
F
C

1979-80
DIVISION TWO

Following a 3-3 draw at Filbert Street in September, Fulham climbed to a season's high of eighth place. Gordon Davies claimed all three of the Cottagers' goals, his second hat-trick in a month. Two of his goals that day against Leicester—a header and a fine opportunist shot—are shown here.

The entertaining draw at Leicester was followed by five consecutive defeats, including one at home to Notts County. Despite a splendid headed goal by Davies (top), an injury to Gerry Peyton saw Kevin Lock (above left) don the keeper's jersey for the first time, and the match was lost 1-3. The gloom that pervaded this stage of the season was lightened only by a surprise victory at Stamford Bridge, with one of the two goals coming from John Beck (above right), and a 1-0 win at Oldham, where Brian Greenaway was on the mark.

The club's first home success for almost three months came in December against Shrewsbury. Tony Gale scored a fine goal in the 2-1 win (top opposite), and Gary Peters almost got another (left). The return of Teddy Maybank after injury sparked some hope, but it was not until the end of February that he re-opened his goal account (below left), with a header in a 1-1 draw against Bristol Rovers.

F
F C
1979-80
DIVISION TWO

Perhaps the most unlikely win in 1980 was at Upton Park in March. A goal by Teddy Maybank (top) was not altogether unexpected, but two by central defender Geoff Banton were a complete surprise. His second is shown at right. There was something of a revival in the closing weeks, but the Cottagers left it too late. Gordon Davies earned a point with a goal at Wrexham (below), the club with which he ended his League career.

Gordon Davies found the target again at home to Newcastle in April, for the only goal of the game. In the picture, top, Gordon is the second player from right. There was some doubt whether his header, which cannoned downwards from the bar, had actually crossed the line, but close inspection of shadows in the photograph confirm it was a good goal. A few days later Ray Lewington headed his first goal for the club in the 2-1 win over Cardiff.

DIVISION TWO 1979-80 Final League Table

		P	W	D	L	F	A	Pts
1	Leicester	42	21	13	8	58	38	55
2	Sunderland	42	21	12	9	69	42	54
3	Birmingham	42	21	11	10	58	38	53
4	Chelsea	42	23	7	12	66	52	53
5	QPR	42	18	13	11	75	53	49
6	Luton	42	16	17	9	66	45	49
7	West Ham	42	20	7	15	54	43	47
8	Cambridge	42	14	16	12	61	53	44
9	Newcastle	42	15	14	13	53	49	44
10	Preston	42	12	19	11	56	52	43
11	Oldham	42	16	11	15	49	53	43
12	Swansea	42	17	9	16	48	53	43
13	Shrewsbury	42	18	5	19	60	53	41
14	Orient	42	12	17	13	48	54	41
15	Cardiff	42	16	8	18	41	48	40
16	Wrexham	42	16	6	20	40	49	38
17	Notts County	42	11	15	16	51	52	37
18	Watford	42	12	13	17	39	46	37
19	Bristol Rovers	42	11	13	18	50	64	35
20	**Fulham**	**42**	**11**	**7**	**24**	**42**	**74**	**29**
21	Burnley	42	6	15	21	39	73	27
22	Charlton	42	6	10	26	39	78	22

Season 1980-81

DIVISION THREE

This was a season of transition at the Cottage, as Bobby Campbell's four-year tenure came to an end, and Malcolm Macdonald took over. A run of six consecutive defeats in September and October saw Fulham drift down the Third Division table and cost Campbell his job. Macdonald, who was working on the commercial side at the club, took over, but he was no overnight success. Working with the players he inherited, he brought in only coach Roger Thompson to replace Mike

Back row: Roger Thompson (coach), Clive Day, Kevin Lock, Gary Peters, Steve Hatter, Tony Gale, Doug Hatcher, Perry Digweed, Roger Brown, Geoff Banton, Tony Mahoney, Ron Woolnough (physio); front: Malcolm Macdonald (manager), John Beck, Sean O'Driscoll, Gordon Davies, Les Strong, Brian Corner, Brian Gibson, Tommy Mason, Robert Wilson.

Kelly, who had left with Campbell. Although morale seemed to improve, results were erratic. It was only in the final weeks that the threat of the Fourth Division was mathematically removed. Macdonald was not afraid to experiment and a number of youngsters were given an opportunity in difficult circumstances. In goal, Jim Stannard made an impressive start, and it was late in the campaign that Jeff Hopkins and Paul Parker made their debuts. Up front, Davies was a lone wanderer and was the only player to get his goal tally into double figures. However, with eight games to go, Dean Coney came into the side, and almost immediately forged an effective understanding with him.

Somehow, the season, although indifferent, ended rather better that many had feared around the New Year. With little money available to strengthen his squad, it was not clear how the new manager was going to turn the club around, but confidence was never a characteristic that Malcolm Macdonald lacked.

This page: Tony Mahoney climbs high against Brentford at Griffin Park, one of only four Fulham victories in the first 15 matches of the season. Against Blackpool at home, Gordon Davies scored, but the Cottagers still lost 1-2. Goalkeeper Gerry Peyton saw plenty of action in the autumn of 1980, and attracted the close attention of opposing forwards.

On the day Bobby Campbell left the club, Fulham faced Millwall at the Cottage and drew 1-1, Gordon Davies getting Fulham's goal (top opposite). A run of seven games without a win was ended in October by another Davies goal, this time at Chester (right). Shortly afterwards, Malcolm Macdonald was appointed manager, and he in turn made Les Strong his skipper.

F F C

1980-81
DIVISION THREE

191

In an entertaining home draw against
Chesterfield in November, the
Cottagers' goal (above) was well taken
by Robert Wilson, at right in the
photograph.

Gordon Davies was the only Fulham
player to reach a double figure goal
tally in the season. Of his 18 League
goals, two came in the drawn game
against Huddersfield in December;
perhaps he might have scored a hat-
trick, had he not been required to
contend with congratulations from
Gary Peters (left).

Roger Brown's goalscoring feats
were still largely to come. One of his
first goals for the club came at Hull in
April 1981 and won the three points.

MATCH OF THE SEASON
Blackpool 0 Fulham 2
14th February 1981

In the late 1980s the Fourth Division was rather too close for comfort for Fulham supporters, and it was a threat that hung over the Cottage for the best part of two seasons. At the start of 1981, however, it was a unique experience to contemplate life in the League's basement, but until this victory at Bloomfield Road, it was a very real prospect.

Manager Malcolm Macdonald was still in the early months of his reign when the team travelled to fellow strugglers Blackpool, managed by his old friend Alan Ball. (Fears that when these two lively characters got together it would result in a manager being sent home in disgrace by the players mercifully proved unfounded.) Without an away win in the League under Macdonald and just one point away from the relegation places, Fulham faced the Seasiders without influential midfielder Ray Lewington and with keeper Jim Stannard making only his

third appearance. On the day, the club got the result it needed. Fulham dominated the opening 30 minutes, and Tony Mahoney gave them a precious half-time lead (above). Although Blackpool came back strongly, Ronnie Goodlass clinched the points in the closing minutes with his second, and last, goal for the club (below).

With this win, some of the pressure was taken off, and the Cottagers climbed to mid table. Within months, Macdonald was to transform this mediocre squad into an exciting, promotion-winning outfit.

The discovery of Dean Coney was one of the few
encouraging developments in a dismal season. He scored the
winner against Charlton at the Cottage in April 1981 (above
right). Apart from that, there were occasional stylish displays,
like that from Tony Gale at Burnley (top left). Old hand Les
Strong scored his first goal for two years (and his last for the
club) against Reading in the last home match of the season
(above). This fixture marked Paul Parker's League debut, but
despite Strongie's efforts, Fulham lost 1-2.

DIVISION THREE 1980-81 Final League Table							
	P	W	D	L	F	A	Pts
1 Rotherham	46	24	13	9	62	32	61
2 Barnsley	46	21	17	8	72	45	59
3 Charlton	46	25	9	12	63	44	59
4 Huddersfield	46	21	14	11	71	40	56
5 Chesterfield	46	23	10	13	72	48	56
6 Portsmouth	46	22	9	15	55	47	53
7 Plymouth	46	19	14	13	56	44	52
8 Burnley	46	18	14	14	60	48	50
9 Brentford	46	14	19	13	52	49	47
10 Reading	46	18	10	18	62	62	46
11 Exeter	46	16	13	17	62	66	45
12 Newport	46	15	13	18	64	61	43
13 **Fulham**	**46**	**15**	**13**	**18**	**57**	**64**	**43**
14 Oxford	46	13	17	16	39	47	43
15 Gillingham	46	12	18	16	48	58	42
16 Millwall	46	14	14	18	43	60	42
17 Swindon	46	13	15	18	51	56	41
18 Chester	46	15	11	20	41	48	41
19 Carlisle	46	14	13	19	57	70	41
20 Walsall	46	13	15	18	59	74	41
21 Sheff United	46	14	13	19	65	62	40
22 Colchester	46	14	11	21	45	65	39
23 Blackpool	46	9	14	23	45	75	32
24 Hull	46	8	16	22	40	71	32

SEASON 1981-82

DIVISION THREE

For the second time in a little over ten years, Fulham climbed out of Division Three after two seasons. It was a merited success, although, in the end, it relied on a nailbiting finale. In his first full season as manager, Malcolm Macdonald had fashioned a side which had cost the club no extra money, and which not only deserved promotion but also played with a flair and a verve that were in the best traditions of the club.

During the summer, former Arsenal winger George Armstrong had succeeded Roger Thompson as coach, and Ray Harford had come on board from Colchester to work with the juniors. The squad was strengthened by the addition of midfielder Peter O'Sullivan, a free transfer from Brighton, whilst Coney, Lewington and Hopkins established themselves in the side at the expense of Mahoney, Beck and Peters. After a shaky start, the team started to gel in the autumn. A run of five wins, climaxed by a 1-0 victory over challengers Chesterfield at the end of January put Fulham on top of the table. This win came from a Gordon Davies goal, one of the most remarkable seen in recent times at the Cottage.

As the season wore on, the three promotion places were being contested by four clubs. Fulham had produced some indifferent results in late April and early May, and promotion depended on the final night of the season. Fulham, needing a point, were at home to Lincoln, who wanted a win. After 90 fiercely contested

Back row: John Reeves, Tony Finnigan, Peter Scott, Clive Day, Steve Tapley, Jeff Hopkins, Dean Coney, Tony Mahoney, Mark Aspinall, Dale Tempest; standing: Steve Hatter, Gary Peters, Robert Wilson, Dave Clement, Jim Stannard, Gerry Peyton, Geoff Banton, Sean O'Driscoll, Kevin Lock, Brian Greenaway, Ray Harford (coach); seated: Peter O'Sullivan, Ray Lewington, Tony Gale, George Armstrong (coach), Les Strong, Malcolm Macdonald (manager), Roger Brown, John Beck, Gordon Davies; front: John Marshall, Brian Cottington, Cliff Carr, Paul Parker, Fernando Varadi, Wayne Kerrins.

minutes, Fulham had gained the point they required in a 1-1 draw.

Over the 46 matches, Davies once again proved a consistent striker, and in Coney found the ideal partner. At the back, Roger Brown was magnificent alongside the stylish Gale and he finished third highest scorer. The side was young enough to raise expectations that a prolonged period of success was at hand.

F^FC

FFC
1981-82
DIVISION THREE

Fulham took time to establish their promotion credentials in 1981-82. When Gordon Davies scored in the 3-1 home win over Newport in October (right), the Cottagers were in 15th position. A key factor in the promotion success was the goalscoring prowess of central defender Roger Brown. This goal in the 1-1 home draw against Walsall in November was the third of 12 he scored in the League that season.

Turf Moor has never been one of Fulham's happiest hunting grounds, and a 2-2 draw against promotion rivals Burnley was a satisfactory result. Gordon Davies scored both goals; his second, a header, is shown above.

An influential but underrated figure in midfield was Peter O'Sullivan. His only goal (right) was worth three points, at Griffin Park in January. The following week, Fulham went top of the table for the first time when they beat Chesterfield 1-0, thanks to one of the most memorable goals seen at the Cottage. Gordon Davies raced 40 yards on to a Brown pass and reached the ball a split second before the goalkeeper who had rushed out to the edge of the penalty area. Gordon shot and the ball duly swished between the posts.

FFC
1981-82
DIVISION THREE

198

Opposite page: In February, West London neighbours, Wimbledon, gave Fulham a fright, but these two goals by Dean Coney helped the Cottagers to the three points in a 4-1 win.

Huddersfield provided unexpectedly resilient opposition at the Cottage in February. Despite goals by Dean Coney (top) and Kevin Lock from the penalty spot, the Terriers came back to draw. The following week, Fulham went to Wales and won 3-1 at Newport, thanks in part to a goal by Robert Wilson.

Opposite: The aerial power of Roger Brown and the striking touch of Sean O'Driscoll were on hand when they mattered most. In the closing weeks of the season, Brown scored twice in the 4-1 win at home to Carlisle (his first goal is shown in the picture), and O'Driscoll scored the goal which earned a point at Walsall.

Brown and O'Driscoll were both on the mark with fine goals in the emphatic 4-2 home win over Bristol Rovers in April.

F F C
1981-82
DIVISION THREE

In the closing weeks, young Dale Tempest showed his potential in several positions. Primarily a striker, he scored a vital goal in Fulham's 2-0 win at Chester in May (above). The penultimate home match was against Preston, which the Cottagers won 3-0, Coney and Davies being the marksmen. Dean Coney's goal is shown below, whilst the Welsh Terrier's second goal (bottom) was a superb strike after an excellent build-up.

MATCH OF THE SEASON
Fulham 1 Lincoln City 1
18th May 1982

On a warm spring evening, Fulham kept a 20,398 crowd on tenterhooks as the Third Division promotion race came to a tense and dramatic climax. With just one game left, four clubs were in contention for three promotion places, and two of them were on duty at the Cottage. The Cottagers needed only a draw to return to Division Two, whilst nothing less than a win would do for the Imps.

The home side's hero was skipper Roger Brown. Undeterred by a cut eye, he was a rock in defence, and for the 12th time that season, got forward to score a crucial goal. It came in the 58th minute. Lincoln defender Steve Thompson was sent off for a second bookable offence, and from Tony Gale's free-kick, Brown soared above the Imps defence to head home a truly memorable goal (above). The ten men of Lincoln fought back, and equalised through David Carr after 72 minutes. Despite some nerve-racking moments in the final quarter of an hour, including a goalline clearance by O'Driscoll, Fulham held on for a promotion that was perhaps more deserved than the point they managed to win that evening.

There was much celebration on the Cottage balcony after the promotion-winning draw against Lincoln City, and many spectators stayed on that night to cheer their heroes.

DIVISION THREE 1981-82 Final League Table

		P	W	D	L	F	A	Pts
1	Burnley	46	21	17	8	66	49	80
2	Carlisle	46	23	11	12	65	50	80
3	**Fulham**	**46**	**21**	**15**	**10**	**77**	**51**	**78**
4	Lincoln	46	21	14	11	66	40	77
5	Oxford	46	19	14	13	63	49	71
6	Gillingham	46	20	11	15	64	56	71
7	Southend	46	18	15	13	63	51	69
8	Brentford	46	19	11	16	56	47	68
9	Millwall	46	18	13	15	62	62	67
10	Plymouth	46	18	11	17	64	56	65
11	Chesterfield	46	18	10	18	67	58	64
12	Reading	46	17	11	18	67	75	62
13	Portsmouth	46	14	19	13	56	51	61
14	Preston	46	16	13	17	50	56	61
15	Bristol Rovers*	46	18	9	19	58	65	61
16	Newport	46	14	16	16	54	54	58
17	Huddersfield	46	15	12	19	64	59	57
18	Exeter	46	16	9	21	71	84	57
19	Doncaster	46	13	17	16	55	68	56
20	Walsall	46	13	14	19	51	55	53
21	Wimbledon	46	14	11	21	61	75	53
22	Swindon	46	13	13	20	55	71	52
23	Bristol City	46	11	13	22	40	65	46
24	Chester	46	7	11	28	36	78	32

*Two points deducted by Football League.

SEASON 1982-83

DIVISION TWO

For much of 1982-83 it seemed that Fulham would repeat their promotion success of the previous season and reclaim the place in the top flight that they had lost 15 years earlier. At the beginning of March, they were in third place, eight points clear of Leicester with 13 games to go, one more than the Filbert Street club. Yet it all went horribly wrong in the closing weeks. The season ended in controversy, with Fulham believing they had been badly mistreated by the authorities. Since then the club has struggled both on and off the field.

The season opened with Ray Harford replacing George Armstrong as coach, and free signing Ray Houghton taking over from Peter O'Sullivan in midfield. Les Strong made way for Kevin Lock at left-back and for Roger Brown as skipper, and within weeks the team slipped into top gear. Away from home, they recorded some remarkable victories, none more so than a stunning 4-1 win at Newcastle, manager Macdonald's old club. Goals by Davies and Houghton that day figured in the top three in BBC's Goal of the Season competition. The Cottagers also put four past Middlesbrough at Ayresome, despite having Kevin Lock in goal for all but the first five minutes and going one down early on; four goals were also scored against Grimsby at Blundell Park and Wolves at Molineux.

Around the New Year, however, goals began to dry up. Although Davies continued to find the net regularly, Dean Coney hit a barren patch and the side started to

Back: Jeff Hopkins, Dale Tempest, Sean O'Driscoll, Kevin Lock, Dean Coney; centre: Brian Greenaway, Steve Hatter, Gerry Peyton, Roger Brown, Jim Stannard, Tony Gale, Robert Wilson, Paul Parker; front: Ray Harford (coach), Ray Lewington, Ray Houghton, Les Strong, Malcolm Macdonald (manager), Peter O'Sullivan, John Reeves, Gordon Davies, Derek Wright (physio).

struggle. A loss at home to Leicester in April by the only goal of the game was to prove critical, although it was the 0-1 defeat at Derby on the last day that angered Fulham and most neutral observers. With a couple of minutes remaining, a crowd invasion forced the referee to 'abandon' the match, and, despite an inquiry, the result was allowed to stand. The arguments surrounding the match would have been academic, however, had the Cottagers not let a 3-0 lead at Barnsley in October become a 3-4 deficit. Promotion was probably lost then.

Fulham played their best football in the first half of the season. In September, Ray Lewington's blistering long-range strike was worth a point against much-fancied QPR, whilst Dean Coney scored spectacular goals in the wins over Bolton and Leeds.

1982-83
DIVISION TWO

In January 1983, it took a Robert Wilson penalty to break down a dour Middlesbrough defence. His first shot (top left) was saved but he followed up to score (top right). A month later, two home points were dropped in a 2-2 draw with Newcastle, despite this fine headed goal by Gordon Davies.

Much of the credit for turning Fulham around in under two years went to manager Malcolm Macdonald (seen here holding his Manager of the Month prize), and his highly regarded coach, Ray Harford.

As the promotion pressure mounted, victories became more elusive. The visit to the Cottage of Grimsby in March 1983 brought Fulham a welcome three points. Man-of-the-match Robert Wilson scored twice (his second is pictured above), and Ray Lewington once (left), in an emphatic 4-0 win. Crystal Palace were also victims at the Cottage that month, falling to a Roger Brown goal. Robert Wilson, Gordon Davies, Jeff Hopkins and Dean Coney share the scorer's joy.

F F C
1982-83
DIVISION TWO

Skipper Brown was again Fulham's
saviour with the winner against
Charlton in April. A week later,
Ray Houghton stunned the 24,328
crowd at Elland Road (below), with
a dramatic last-gasp equaliser against
Leeds.

MATCH OF THE SEASON
Fulham 0   Leicester City 1
23rd April 1983

If the recent history of Fulham F.C. has turned on the result of a single match, then this was it. From October onwards, the Cottagers were in top place in Division Three and looked a safe bet to secure a second promotion in twelve months. After the turn of the year, however, points began to slip away, whilst Leicester, in fourth place, were closing the gap. The importance of this meeting of the two clubs was apparent from the outset, for it attracted the season's best gate to the Cottage—24,257.

With Gary Lineker and Alan Smith leading the attack, Leicester came looking for the three points, but it was their Scottish player Ian Wilson who scored the only goal. He shot from 15 yards in the 63rd minute whilst the home defence stood off. It might have been so very different had a Gordon Davies 'goal' (above) not been disallowed for offside. The referee at first appeared to give the goal but then saw the linesman flagging. Towards the end of the match, when Dean Coney missed from close range (below), Fulham knew it was not going to be their day, though in the event a draw would have been enough to put Fulham up.

Malcolm Macdonald's promising young side was broken up within two years, and within another year the club found itself in the Third Division.

Above: a consolation goal for Fulham on Easter Monday on the Loftus Road plastic came from Gordon Davies who broke the QPR offside trap in the 1-3 defeat.

The controversial finale against Derby at the Baseball Ground in May (remaining pictures) began in smiles and spring sunshine. Gordon Davies featured in most of Fulham's best attacking moves. However, a crowd invasion brought the proceedings to a premature conclusion, when the referee 'abandoned' the match with a couple of minutes to go. The score of 1-0 to Derby was allowed to stand.

The find of the season for Fulham was Ray Houghton, a free transfer signing from West Ham. He established himself in the side with some dazzling midfield displays and a few highly individual goals. Here he celebrates in typical fashion the goal which clinched the home win over Burnley in October.

DIVISION TWO 1982-83 Final League Table							
	P	W	D	L	F	A	Pts
1 QPR	42	26	7	9	77	36	85
2 Wolves	42	20	15	7	68	44	75
3 Leicester	42	20	10	12	72	44	70
4 **Fulham**	**42**	**20**	**9**	**13**	**64**	**47**	**69**
5 Newcastle	42	18	13	11	75	53	67
6 Sheff Wed	42	16	15	11	60	47	63
7 Oldham	42	14	19	9	64	47	61
8 Leeds	42	13	21	8	51	46	60
9 Shrewsbury	42	15	14	13	48	48	59
10 Barnsley	42	14	15	13	57	57	57
11 Blackburn	42	15	12	15	58	58	57
12 Cambridge	42	13	12	17	42	60	51
13 Derby	42	10	19	13	49	58	49
14 Carlisle	42	12	12	18	68	70	48
15 Crystal Palace	42	12	12	18	43	52	48
16 Middlesbrough	42	11	15	16	46	67	48
17 Charlton	42	13	9	20	63	86	48
18 Chelsea	42	11	14	17	51	61	47
19 Grimsby	42	12	11	19	45	70	47
20 Rotherham	42	10	15	17	45	68	45
21 Burnley	42	12	8	22	56	66	44
22 Bolton	42	11	11	20	42	61	44

CUP DRAMAS 1958-83

T he two major Cup competitions—the F.A. Cup and the Football League Cup (which began in 1960)—provided only intermittently the sort of excitement that was regularly on offer in the promotion and relegation battles in the League. There were, nevertheless, moments of matchless drama in this quarter of a century of Cup football which were the equal of any high or low point in the Cottagers' entire history.

Some records were established. Maurice Cook's goal at Eastville in the League Cup in September 1960 was the first ever in the competition. Sadly, there appears to have been no photographer amongst the 20,022 crowd to record the event. When Fulham lost in the semi-final of the F.A. Cup to

Burnley in 1962, they became the only club to appear in four semi-finals of the competition without at least once reaching the final. Happily the next time the Cottagers got that far, in 1975, they at last reached Wembley, though it took them 11 matches to do so, the longest journey ever (and every tie was won away from home).

This section of the book illustrates some of the highlights of the club's Cup exploits in these years. Almost inevitably, Fulham's successes came when they were cast in the role of underdogs. Even as a First Division side, their best Cup performances came when they were stranded at the foot of the table and found some relief in the knock-out competitions.

Between January 1958 and December 1983, Fulham played 53 F.A. Cup ties (78 matches including replays) and 51 League Cup ties (78 matches). In the following pages, some of the memorable moments are recalled, and some of the memorable stories are retold.

Johnny Haynes shows his frustration in the League Cup tie against Leeds in September 1969, typifying the Maestro's Cup fortunes during his long Fulham career.

Fulham took two games to beat Charlton in the fourth round of the Cup in January 1958. In the replay at the Valley, Charlton centre-forward Ryan headed past Macedo into the net (above), only for the goal to be disallowed. Had it stood, Fulham's Cup run might have gone no further.

In a five-goal thriller at Upton Park in the fifth round, the Cottagers edged out West Ham. Left: Macedo, Cohen and Langley thwart a Hammers attack. Below: Tosh Chamberlain runs to celebrate Haynes's winning goal, whilst John Bond lies dejectedly on the ground.

In front of an all-ticket 42,000 crowd at the Cottage, Fulham won through to the semi-finals for the third time by beating Bristol Rovers, with the three goals shown opposite, from Jimmy Hill and Arthur Stevens (2).

In an emotionally charged semi-final at Villa Park against the post-Munich Busby Babes, Fulham came back from behind to lead Manchester United, but were eventually held to a 2-2 draw. Arthur Stevens equalised Bobby Charlton's early goal with a shot that had Gregg well beaten (top). Then Jimmy Hill put the Cottagers ahead (above), maintaining his record of scoring in every round. One of the heroes of the day was Fulham keeper Macedo. In the picture on the right he denies Webster, watched by Joe Stapleton (No. 5) and a young George Cohen.

216

Once again Fulham's progress in the Cup ended one step short of Wembley when United won the semi-final replay 5-3 at Highbury. United forward Alex Dawson, who got a hat-trick, opened the scoring with a diving header (left). Fulham hit back with (below) goals from Arthur Stevens (the last of his 124 for the club) and Tosh Chamberlain.

F.A. CUP
1957-58
continued

Seconds after Fulham thought they had come back to 4-4 (but the 'goal' was disallowed), United broke away and clinched the tie with their fifth goal, from Charlton. The picture above shows the extremes of emotion felt by the two sides.

The Cup run marked the introduction to top-class football of goalkeeper Tony Macedo (right). He was still doing his National Service with the RAF at the time. Below: manager Dug Livingstone shares a joke with most of the other players in the Cup squad: Jimmy Hill, George Cohen, Arthur Stevens, Johnny Haynes, Robin Lawler, Joe Stapleton, Roy Dwight, Eddie Lowe and Tosh Chamberlain.

The Cup run in 1961-62 began with a comfortable 3-1 home win over Fourth Division Hartlepools. The top picture shows Cook slotting home the first of his two goals. Fulham were given a fright in the fourth round, needing a replay to overcome Second Division Walsall. A Richards penalty (above) put the Saddlers ahead in the first match at the Cottage, but Fulham came back to draw. Third Division Port Vale proved just as stubborn in the fifth round. Despite the efforts of Henderson (left), it took a fine display by Macedo (below) and a controversial late penalty from Langley to see the Cottagers through.

Against First Division opponents for the first time in their 1961-62 Cup run, Fulham came back from 0-2 down to draw 2-2 with Blackburn Rovers at the Cottage. Several Fulham attacks were blunted by Fred Else (left), but Fulham would have won at the first attempt had Langley converted a spot-kick (centre picture opposite). In the replay at Ewood Park, a Maurice Cook goal, shown at the bottom of the opposite page, was all that separated the two teams.

The Cottagers were desperately unlucky not to beat favourites Burnley at Villa Park in the semi-final. They took the lead through Graham Leggat with a shot that left goalkeeper Blacklaw helpless (right). Leggat came close to adding a second (below) before Burnley equalised to force a replay. At Filbert Street in the second game, the Clarets probably shaded it, and won 2-1. Macedo was the busier of the two keepers; in the picture at the foot of the page, he saves brilliantly from Connelly.

F.A. CUP
1962-63

A memorable photograph from an unmemorable goalless draw with West Ham in the third round of the F.A. Cup in February 1963. This was the club's first match of the year following the 'Big Freeze'.

LEAGUE CUP
1966-67

The League Cup was not particularly fruitful for Fulham in the 1960s. An exception was the 5-0 victory over Wolves in October 1966; the goals, shown in the following pictures, came from Earle, Clarke, Conway, Clarke again, and Barrett.

F F C
LEAGUE CUP
1967-68

The furthest Fulham have progressed in the League Cup is the last eight. This was first achieved in the dreadful League season of 1967-68. It took a replay to beat humble Workington in the third round, but Fulham made no mistake at the Cottage winning 6-2. Les Barrett was on the mark that evening (right), but the highlight was four goals from Allan Clarke, shown below scoring his second.

In the fourth round, Fulham scored an unexpected win over that season's League champions Manchester City, 3-2 at the Cottage. In the picture below, originally taken as an experiment on colour film, Steve Earle can just be seen scoring the second of his two goals.

A semi-final place seemed likely when Joe Gilroy scored against Huddersfield in the fourth round (above), his late goal cancelling out the visitors' first-half lead. Unfortunately, the Terriers won the replay.

F F
C

F.A. CUP
1967-68

In the F.A. Cup in 1967-68, struggling Fulham were lucky to overcome non-League Macclesfield Town. The turning-point, shown below, was Allan Clarke's penalty kick, which Steve Earle (No. 8) could not bear to watch.

There was another trip to the League Cup quarter-finals for Fulham in 1970-71. The most impressive wins for the Third Division Cottagers came in October against Second Division QPR, when Les Barrett was one of the two marksmen, and against Swindon, also of Division Two, beaten by a Steve Earle goal.

West London rivals QPR were also
Fulham's victims the following
season, this time in the F.A. Cup in
January 1972. It took two games to
settle the tie. The first game at
Loftus Road was drawn 1-1, thanks
to Jimmy Conway's long-range
goal, and in the replay, the
Cottagers won 2-1, both goals
coming from Roger Cross. His
winning goal is shown below.

F F C
LEAGUE CUP
1974-75

The 1974-75 season was Fulham's outstanding Cup season. It started with a victory in the League Cup second round at Wolves. The First Division club fell to goals by Les Barrett, Viv Busby, and Les Barrett again; Wolves scored just once in reply.

In the fourth round in October 1974, Fulham met West Ham for the first of
two Cup meetings that season. Long-range efforts by the two Alans
—Mullery (above), and Slough (below)—put the Cottagers through to a tie
at Newcastle, where the Wembley dream faded. The No. 6 in the West Ham
team was Kevin Lock, later to make a big impact playing for Fulham.

F.A. CUP
1974-75

After the disappointments of 1958 and 1962 (not to mention 1908 and 1936), Fulham struck Wembley gold in the F.A. Cup of 1975. It was a long tortuous road, with every tie won away from home. It took three games to overcome Hull in the third round. Jim Conway's header at the Cottage (above) was cancelled by Wagstaffe's late equaliser. Although Viv Busby scored twice at Boothferry Park (below), so did the Tigers, and the third game moved to Filbert Street.

Alan Slough's goal (above) finally saw off Hull, but it only set up an even
longer saga with Brian Clough's Nottingham Forest. After a goalless draw at
the Cottage at the end of January, John Dowie's goal gave Fulham the lead
at the City Ground (below), but Forest equalised, and when extra time failed
to settle the tie, the third game went back to the Cottage, Fulham having
won the toss for the venue. Fulham took the lead through Alan Slough
(bottom), but again Forest equalised, and the fourth meeting in 13 days (with
a couple of other League matches in between) was at Nottingham.

F^FC
F.A. CUP
1974-75
continued

*Viv Busby was the hero of Fulham's seventh match
in that season's F.A. Cup. He touched in Jimmy
Conway's cross to put the visitors one up in the
second match at City Ground (pictures below).*

In the second half, as the mists from the Trent swirled around the ground, Busby took the ball from the centre circle, ran at the defence, rounded the keeper and scored from an acute angle (pictures above). Although Chapman reduced the arrears, the Cottagers held on for a visit to First Division leaders Everton five days later. A sensational victory at Goodison gave Fulham fans serious thoughts about Wembley. Again Busby was the man of the moment. When Everton's keeper Davies fumbled a Jimmy Conway cross (below left), Viv crashed the ball into the net from about 18 inches.

Everton equalised through Kenyon in the second half, but Busby restored Fulham's advantage with a glorious goal that made him an instant Cottage legend. Fastening on to yet another Jimmy Conway pull-back, he hammered the ball into the net to secure a famous victory.

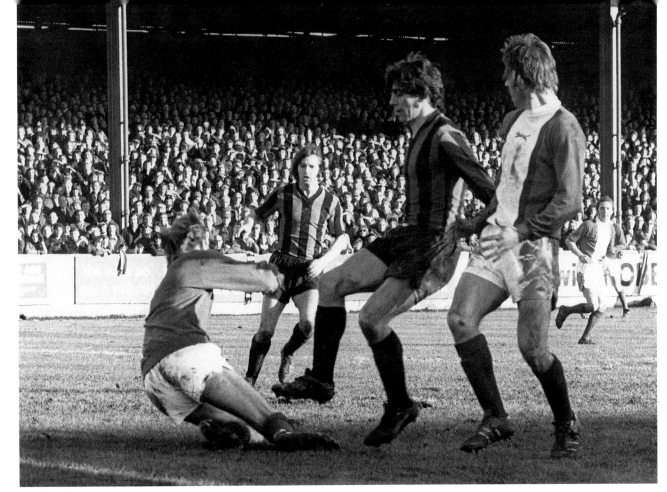

The quarter-finals in March paired Fulham with First Division Carlisle at Brunton Park. It was a hard-earned win for the Londoners, and came from a defensive mix-up. The goalkeeper and full-back hesitated over a Busby cross, Jimmy Conway nipped in (above), and in the confusion, the ball fell to Les Barrett who gratefully prodded it in (left). At the other end, Peter Mellor had his most memorable game for Fulham, making several magnificent saves, such as the one captured from TV. He earned the cigar and champagne that he shared with scorer Barrett on the return journey.

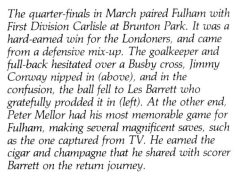

It was Hillsborough rather than unlucky Villa Park for the semi-final in April, but the jinx still appeared to be on Fulham's Wembley ambitions. John Mitchell's second-half goal (left) deserved to win any match, but Gallagher put Birmingham City back on terms and took the tie to Maine Road.

Mitch was again on the mark in the replay, but on this occasion he made sure there was no time left for the Blues to come back. His opportunist effort came in the last minute of extra time, and although it was a scrappy goal, as the pictures show, the crowded Fulham dressing-room afterwards was celebrating the quantity rather than the quality. After four previous semi-final failures, and 11 F.A. Cup games in 1975, the Cottagers had at last made it through to the final.

F F C

**F.A. CUP
1974-75
WEMBLEY**

The Wembley squad. Back row: John Collins (coach), Ron Woolnough (physio), Barry Lloyd, Les Strong, Ernie Howe, John Lacy, Peter Mellor, John Dowie, Viv Busby, John Mitchell, John Fraser, Bill Taylor (chief coach); front: Jimmy Conway, Alan Slough, Alan Mullery, Alec Stock (manager), Bobby Moore, Les Barrett, John Cutbush.

On the road to Wembley!

Right: A smiling and relaxed Alec Stock leads out his Fulham team.

First-half action as Alan Slough moves on to a pass, and Hammers' Frank Lampard closes in to challenge.

F^FC

F.A. CUP
1974-75
WEMBLEY

Jimmy Conway and Les Barrett try to find ways through the Hammers' defence.

Below: A great shot from John Mitchell is brilliantly saved by Mervyn Day, and it looks as though it's not going to be Fulham's day.

Indeed, it isn't Fulham's day, and it ends in defeat but not disgrace. Chairman Tommy Trinder looks justifiably proud as he congratulates skipper Alan Mullery from the Royal Box.

Bill Taylor looks disconsolate; Viv Busby acknowledges the applause of the Fulham fans; in spite of the defeat, it had been a great day.

It was another four years before Fulham enjoyed Cup
excitement against higher division clubs. In the third round of
the F.A. Cup in January 1979, the Cottagers beat First Division
QPR 2-0 at the Cottage. John Margerrison falls as he hits the
ball past Phil Parkes for Fulham's first goal (above), and the
second came from razor-sharp Gordon Davies who fastened on
to a right-wing cross to score from six yards.

The fourth round brought Manchester United to the Cottage.
John Margerrison's superb headed goal (above) was meagre
reward for all Fulham's pressure, but it earned a draw. At Old
Trafford, Jimmy Greenhoff's shot was deflected past Gerry
Peyton for the only goal of the game. The visitors had their
moments, and even Ray Evans went up to support the attack.

The Third Division promotion season of 1981-82 also saw some
impressive League Cup results. Second Division Newcastle were
beaten in both legs of the second round in October 1981, by 2-1
at St. James', the goals (above) coming from Robert Wilson and
Dean Coney, and by 2-0 at the Cottage with a Ray Lewington
penalty opening the scoring.

The second goal in the home victory against Newcastle (top) came from a Dean Coney slide-in.

In the third round in November, Fulham travelled to Second Division Oldham and emerged with a creditable 1-1 draw, the goal scored by Robert Wilson and set up by Gordon Davies.

In the Oldham replay, there was only one team in it. Dean Coney and Jeff Hopkins put Fulham two up very early in the first half, Hopkins with his first-ever goal.

Oldham's fate was sealed in the second half with a magnificent
headed goal by Dean Coney. The reward was a trip to White
Hart Lane in December for the fourth round. Despite having
much of the play, Fuham lost out to a Mike Hazard goal, and
Spurs went on to the final at Wembley. In the picture below,
Coney and Roberts dispute possession, whilst Gordon Davies is
on hand for the loose ball.

FFC
LEAGUE CUP
1983-84

An indifferent season sprang to life in November 1983 with three fiercely contested third round League Cup matches against holders Liverpool; the tie was settled only in extra time of the third game by a mis-hit shot from Graeme Souness.

Kevin Lock kept his nerve to score from the spot in the first game (above), after Gordon Davies had been fouled.

Below, in the replay at Anfield, John Marshall, in his first full season in the side, takes on the experienced Alan Kennedy.

More pictures from the Anfield replay.

Paul Parker protects his keeper Gerry Peyton from the marauding Kenny Dalglish. Parker was later carried off injured.

Kevin Lock coolly puts his penalty kick in the same spot as he did in the first match; but, as Gary Pearce's dramatic picture shows, Grobbelaar has no chance.

The third match, at the Cottage, went to extra time, and
the players needed their drinks and the magic sponge; but in
the end, Gordon Davies' diving header was as close as Fulham
came to scoring.

THE PLAYERS

To select Fulham's leading players between 1958 and 1983 on anything but a purely statistical basis would be an exercise in subjectivity that would almost certainly annoy many more people than it would please. Space will only allow for 40 players to be highlighted, and to avoid any arguments about favouritism, these 40 have been selected simply by the number of appearances made in the period. Included in the totals are all League appearances from seasons 1958-59 to 1982-83, as well as all F.A. Cup and League Cup appearances throughout the years 1958 to 1983 inclusive. Any appearances made outside these dates are excluded, and thus Les Barrett rather than Johnny Haynes tops the list since 216 of the Maestro's games came in earlier years. The full list of 40 players in order of appearances is given below. The dates are when the players first joined, and finally left, the club, but do not go beyond the years covered by this book.

1	Les Barrett	(1966-77)	491
2	Johnny Haynes	(1958-70)	441
3	George Cohen	(1958-69)	432
4	Les Strong	(1972-82)	427
5	Alan Mullery	(1959-76)	412
6	Stan Brown	(1961-72)	397
7	Tony Macedo	(1958-68)	368
8	Jimmy Conway	(1966-76)	360
9	Fred Callaghan	(1964-74)	336
10	Steve Earle	(1964-73)	327
11	Jim Langley	(1958-65)	306
12	Gerry Peyton	(1976-83)	290
13	Barry Lloyd	(1969-76)	289
14	Tony Gale	(1977-83)	281
15	Graham Leggat	(1958-66)	280
16	Gordon Davies	(1978-83)	237
17	Maurice Cook	(1958-65)	233
18	Peter Mellor	(1972-76)	224
19	Bobby Robson	(1962-67)	213
20	John Mitchell	(1972-78)	194
21	John Lacy	(1972-78)	192
22	Eddie Lowe	(1958-63)	190
23	Kevin Lock	(1978-83)	189
24	Alan Slough	(1973-77)	187
25	Johnny Key	(1958-66)	181
26	Reg Matthewson	(1968-72)	174
27	John Dempsey	(1965-69)	171
28	Brian O'Connell	(1958-66)	170
29	Jimmy Dunne	(1970-74)	166
30	Sean O'Driscoll	(1980-83)	160
31	John Cutbush	(1972-77)	160
32	Bobby Moore	(1974-77)	150
33	Roger Brown	(1980-83)	148
34	Viv Busby	(1973-76)	143
35	Robert Wilson	(1980-83)	142
36	Ray Lewington	(1980-83)	127
37	John Beck	(1978-81)	126
38	Bobby Keetch	(1961-66)	120
39	Richard Money	(1977-80)	115
40	Terry Bullivant	(1972-79)	115

Each of the first 20 players has a page to himself, beginning overleaf. The remaining 20 have a half-page each, beginning on page 272. Finally on pages 282 and 283 are portraits of every other Fulham player who made at least 20 appearances for the club during the period covered.

Les Barrett

Les Barrett thrilled the crowds at Craven Cottage for 12 seasons with his exhilarating runs down the left wing using his electric speed. He also scored many memorable goals in the total of 89 that he achieved during 491 appearances for the club. There was always a surge of excitement in the crowd when Les went on one of his runs, often cutting inside to have a shot on goal or to put over a dangerous cross. In his early days at the club, he formed an exciting forward line with Allan Clarke and Steve Earle, and he gained an Under-23 cap for England against Greece in 1967. Les and Jimmy Conway tore Third Division defences to shreds when Fulham clinched promotion in 1970-71, and he also was a member of the F.A. Cup final side in 1975. Les left Fulham in October 1977 for Millwall and later played for California Surf, Carshalton Athletic and Woking. He seems to be amongst the last of a dying breed of flying wingers.

Johnny Haynes

Fulham's greatest player—and one of the outstanding inside-forwards of his generation—Johnny Haynes was capped on 56 occasions, many as skipper. He also gained 'B' caps, eight Under-23 caps, schoolboy honours, and represented the Football League on 13 occasions. He stayed loyal to Fulham despite lucrative offers, but won neither Cup nor League trophies. He easily tops the appearances table with 657 games, and dictated most of them with his magnificent tactical brain, control and passing ability. He scored 157 goals for Fulham; his last, at Brighton in November 1969, is shown below. He was a perfectionist who was as hard on himself as he was on others, and was famous for his withering looks to colleagues when they had not read his play on the field. Johnny signed amateur forms for the club in July 1950 and professional forms in May 1952, his Fulham playing career stretching from December 1952 until January 1970. The Maestro was idolised by the Fulham supporters, and many present-day fans must regret that they never saw him play. A car crash in 1962 ended his international career but his Fulham career lasted for another eight seasons. He was caretaker manager briefly from November 1968. He moved to South Africa in August 1970, and later played for Durban United, Durban Celtic, and Wealdstone briefly in November 1972. He now lives in Edinburgh; his place as a Fulham legend is secure.

George Cohen

George Cohen's finest footballing hour came at Wembley, not the Cottage, when he was a member of the England side which won the World Cup in 1966. One of Fulham's best-ever defenders, he combined razor-sharp tackling with strength and speed. He was able to recover quickly when beaten by an opponent, and loved to support the forwards in attack, though he was marginally better at getting forward than he was at crossing the ball. He gained 37 caps for England, eight caps at Under-23 level, and made four appearances for the Football League. He shared in all Fulham's major successes of the late 1950s and 1960s—two F.A. Cup semi-finals, and promotion to Division One. George rarely missed a match, but a terrible injury received against Liverpool at the Cottage in December 1967, from which he never fully recovered, forced him into retirement in March 1969. George ran Fulham's youth team until 1971, and later managed Tonbridge from March 1974. Today he runs his own building and property business in the Tonbridge area, after his fight back from serious illness.

Les Strong

Les Strong signed for Fulham as an apprentice in February 1970 and started as a pencil-thin right winger but ended his career as a stocky full-back. A player who could always see the brighter side of life even when the crowd were getting at him, he was the only player to stay with the club throughout Bobby Campbell's years in charge, and probably needed a sense of humour to survive. Les was at his best when playing alongside Bobby Moore in defence, and he played exceptionally well in Fulham's run to Wembley in 1975. Sadly, he missed the final due to an injury received just before the big day, but had a special medal struck for him by the F.A. He missed just four League games between 1976 and 1982, and was ever present in 1981-82 as Fulham clinched promotion back to Division Two. He moved to Brentford in December 1982, and later played for Crystal Palace and Rochdale, but retired in November 1984. The following year he returned to the Cottage as catering manager, but recently he has been coaching a national side in the West Indies. One of the best totally right-footed left-backs around at the time, he played football with a smile. If he ever published a coaching manual, it would contain a lot of original material, much of which might improve the modern game.

Alan Mullery

Alan Mullery had a marvellous career with Fulham, Tottenham Hotspur and England, winning many honours for clubs and country, including 35 caps for England. His finest year with Fulham came in 1975: his inspirational captaincy took the club to the F.A. Cup final; he was voted Footballer of the Year; and he was awarded the M.B.E. Alan joined Fulham as an amateur in June 1957, signing professional forms in December 1958. He became a first-team regular as Fulham clinched promotion to the First Division and also played in the 1962 Cup run. His fierce competitiveness, total commitment, and not inconsiderable skill at wing-half made an enormous contribution to Fulham's First Division survival. It came as a shock when he was sold to Spurs for £72,500 in March 1964. He helped Spurs win the F.A. Cup in 1967, the Football League Cup in 1971, and the EUFA Cup in 1972. When he returned to the Cottage in 1972, he had lost none of his old enthusiasm and he forced the best out of his colleagues. After retiring in May 1976, Alan managed Brighton, Charlton Athletic, Crystal Palace, QPR, Brighton again and Southwick.

Stan Brown

Unobtrusive, ultra reliable and extremely consistent, the perpetually young-looking Stan Brown did a lot of the donkey work which allowed the stars in the side to shine, and he was greatly appreciated by his team-mates. Stan played in just about every position for Fulham except goalkeeper in his 397 appearances for the club in which he scored 19 goals. He was good in the air, an excellent tackler and a good distributor of the ball. Stan scored eight goals in season 1962-63, most of which was spent at centre-forward or inside-left. Near the end of his career, he usually played at the centre of the defence or in midfield. He left Fulham in 1972 and subsequently played for Brighton, Colchester, Wimbledon, and some Sussex League clubs. He retired from playing at 41, a much under-rated player who had given Fulham great service in three divisions of the League.

Tony Macedo

Brave and acrobatic, Tony Macedo was a typical 'continental' goalkeeper, often brilliant but prone to the occasional lapse. Born in Gibraltar, he was the son of a Spanish international. He went to the Cottage in 1954 and signed professional forms in October 1955. He was flown from Germany where he was doing his national service when he first broke into the side in December 1957. In Fulham's two Cup runs of 1958 and 1962, Tony was outstanding, and was the regular keeper when the Cottagers entered the First Division in 1959. Macedo gained ten Under-23 caps, but his later inconsistency meant that he missed out on full honours. The latter part of his career was dogged by injury. He transferred to Colchester United in September 1968 after 391 appearances for Fulham, a total for a Fulham goalkeeper exceeded only by Arthur Reynolds in the years either side of World War One. He later played for Durban City and Highlands Park in South Africa, and still lives in that country today.

Jimmy Conway

*A genial Irishman who played for the club in three
Divisions, Jimmy Conway started his Fulham career as a
wing-half but was later very effective on the right wing,
especially during Fulham's Third Division days. He was
joint top scorer with 23 goals in 1969-70 but as his career
developed, he played in a more withdrawn midfield role.
A versatile player, Jimmy also appeared at right-back for
Fulham. Born in Dublin in October 1946, he came from
a family of 17. His brother John also played for Fulham.
Jimmy gained 19 caps for the Republic of Ireland and
also represented them at schoolboy, youth and amateur
levels. He joined Fulham from Bohemians in May 1966,
and made his first-team debut five months later, scoring
a goal in a League Cup victory over Wolves. He was
unlucky with injuries in the early Seventies but made a
comeback to appear at Wembley in the Cup final in
1975. The following year he moved to Manchester City
for a £30,000 fee. From March 1978, he played for
Portland Timbers in the North American Soccer League.*

Fred Callaghan

A wholehearted player much admired by the Fulham fans, and affectionately nicknamed 'The Tank' because of his surging runs down the left wing, Fred Callaghan joined Fulham as a professional in January 1962. He made his debut in March 1964 after the departure of Alan Mullery to Spurs. Initially a wing-half, he later became the regular left-back. He played a vital role in the club's promotion back to Division Two in 1971. Fred scored few goals, but one at the Valley in April 1972 ultimately sent Charlton down to the Third Division instead of Fulham. A slipped disc during the summer of 1973 virtually ended his career and he retired in May 1974. Fred subsequently managed Enfield, Woking and Brentford, and since late 1991, he has been the manager of Basingstoke. Not the most naturally gifted of individuals, his attitude and commitment nevertheless made him one of the outstanding personalities of his era.

Steve Earle

A fast, skilful striker, Steve Earle scored over 100 goals for Fulham in 11 seasons, in three Divisions for six managers. These included many vital strikes in the Great Escape from relegation in 1965-66, and in Fulham's seasons in Division Three. His five goals in the famous 8-0 victory at Halifax in September 1969 equalled the club record for goals in one League game. He joined the club as an apprentice from school in July 1961 and stayed at the Cottage until he was sold to Leicester City for £70,000 in November 1973 to ease the club's financial pressures. He later played for Peterborough, before moving to the States in 1978 to play for Detroit Express, Tulsa Roughnecks, and finally Wichita Wings. Steve still lives in the U.S.A., and currently coaches at local level with his wife.

Jim Langley

A superb left-back who had a wide range of tricks, such as bicycle kicks, overhead kicks, an enormous throw-in and superb slide tackle, Jim Langley was a great favourite of the Fulham crowd and was noted for his sportsmanship and sense of fun. He turned professional with Guildford City in 1949, and then played for Leeds United and Brighton. He joined Fulham in February 1957 and soon won the first of his three caps for England. He also gained 'B' caps and represented the Football League. After 356 appearances for Fulham he moved on to QPR in July 1965 and helped them to the Third Division title and the Football League Cup in 1967. He became player-manager of Hillingdon Borough in September 1967 and played at Wembley again in 1971 at the age of 42, winning an F.A. Trophy runners-up medal. In 1971, he became a coach at Crystal Palace but soon returned to Hillingdon, staying until their demise in 1985. Since then, Jim has been a steward at the local British Legion Club.

Gerry Peyton

A very consistent goalkeeper, Gerry Peyton possessed fine positional sense and made difficult saves look easy with his anticipation and handling skills. As a youngster he never made the grade at Aston Villa, and drifted into non-League soccer. Burnley saw his potential and signed him in May 1975. He was out of the first team when Fulham bought him in December 1976 for a £35,000 fee, to replace another Burnley old boy, Peter Mellor. He gave the Cottagers excellent service and went on to make 395 appearances before being given a free transfer in July 1986, and moving to join the contingent of Fulham exiles at Bournemouth. Gerry chose to play for the Republic of Ireland rather than England, and has gained 30 caps for his country. He made 238 appearances for Bournemouth before moving to Everton in 1991, but, unable to gain a first-team place, he moved to Norwich City on loan near the end of the 1991-92 season.

Barry Lloyd

Barry Lloyd was captain of Fulham's promotion side of
1971. He was a hard-working midfield player who was the
engine room of the side. He signed professional forms with
Chelsea in February, but was a fringe player, and in
February 1969 he joined Fulham for £35,000 in an exchange
deal which took John Dempsey to the Bridge. Given the
onerous task by manager Bill Dodgin of replacing Johnny
Haynes in the No. 10 shirt and as captain, Lloyd revelled in
the challenge. A regular for most of his time at the Cottage,
he was unlucky to spend Cup final day in 1975 on the
substitute's bench after playing in some of the earlier
rounds. In October 1976, he moved to Hereford United,
and later played for Brentford and Houston Hurricanes in
the States. He managed Yeovil from 1978 to 1981, then
became a successful manager of Worthing. He was
appointed Alan Mullery's assistant at Brighton in May 1986,
and took over himself eight months later. Under him,
Brighton reached runners-up spot in Division Three in 1988.

Tony Gale

Tony Gale played 318 games for Fulham, and yet he was only 24 years old when he moved to West Ham United for £225,000 in August 1984. A skilful and cultured defender, Gale always seemed to make time for himself when in possession. He joined Fulham as an apprentice in 1976 and soon gained England Youth honours and, later, an Under-21 cap. He made his first-team debut at just 16, and in his early years, Fulham used him in midfield as well as defence, where he showed a flair for goalscoring. Tony was a key member of the 1981-82 promotion side, his partnership with Roger Brown at the heart of the defence being the rock on which the team was built. He was unlucky not to win full international honours as he was the classiest of defenders. At Upton Park, he helped West Ham to runners-up spot in Division Two in 1990-91 and also appeared in semi-finals of the League Cup and F.A. Cup. A player in the best Fulham tradition, the decline of the club started with his departure.

Graham Leggat

Arguably, Fulham's best-ever transfer deal was the signing of Graham Leggat from Aberdeen in 1958. A great favourite of the crowd, Leggat was a direct, fast, goalscoring forward who was prepared to play in any position in the forward line. This flexibility probably cost him more Scottish caps but Graham played for his country on 18 occasions and also represented the Scottish League five times. During his time at Aberdeen, Graham scored 92 goals in 151 appearances and gained a League Championship medal in 1955, and two Cup medals. He moved to the Cottage in August 1958 for a mere £15,000 fee. He scored eight hat-tricks for Fulham, including one in three minutes in the 10-1 demolition of Ipswich Town on Boxing Day 1963. This still stands as a First Division record. Graham is also the only Fulham player to have scored a century of First Division goals, a record that will probably stand for all time. He was surprisingly sold to Birmingham City in January 1967 for £20,000 after scoring five goals in his previous two games. In July 1968, he moved to Rotherham, and then took up a coaching post at Aston Villa. He joined Bromsgrove Rovers in March 1970, but moved to Canada in 1971 to become player-manager of Toronto Metros. Recently he has been working for T.S.N. in Ontario as a TV football commentator. He was, unquestionably, one of the best players in Fulham's best-ever side.

Gordon Davies

Gordon Davies holds the goalscoring record for
Fulham with 179 goals in 463 appearances, 159 in
the League and 20 in Cup competitions. He scored
20 or more goals in each of the four seasons from
1980 to 1984. Affectionately known as Ivor by the
fans, Davies, a qualified geography teacher, made
a late entry into League soccer when he joined
Fulham in 1978 from Merthr Tydfil for a bargain
£4,000 at the age of 22. His 18 caps for Wales
included an appearance at Wembley in February
1983 against England. Gordon tried his luck in the
First Division with Chelsea from November 1984,
and the following year moved on to Manchester
City, where he scored regularly. A year later he
returned to the Cottage for a second spell. Gordon
left Fulham finally in August 1991 to join
Wrexham and, after helping them beat Arsenal in
the F.A. Cup, moved to Norway to become
player-manager of Tornado in January 1992.
Always a great crowd favourite, Ivor was the last
of the Cottage heroes, and his goalscoring record
is unlikely to be beaten.

Maurice Cook

A bustling centre-forward who had a nose for goals, Maurice Cook's contribution was often under-rated. He was hard, direct and brave, an old-fashioned centre-forward who maybe lacked speed and control, but who had an abundance of perseverance. He joined Watford in May 1953, for whom he proved a very versatile player, and was picked to represent the Third Division South whilst at Vicarage Road. In February 1958, Cookie signed for Fulham. Cup-tied for their run that season, Maurice played in every game of Fulham's Cup run of 1962. He has the distinction of scoring the first ever goal in the League Cup competition. A regular in the promotion side of 1958-59, he shared the striking duties with Graham Leggat for five First Division seasons. The arrival of new manager Vic Buckingham led to Cook's departure for Reading in May 1965. He later ran a pub in Watford, and today is head of security at the Oval cricket ground.

Peter Mellor

The blond-haired Mellor was an eccentric but effective keeper who was admired by the Fulham supporters. He was at his best in Fulham's F.A. Cup run to Wembley in 1975. Although he had a disappointing game in the final itself, he took much of the credit for the team's progress during the previous 11 matches. Initially an apprentice with Manchester City, he was released and joined Witton Albion, but moved to Burnley in April 1969. Mellor was given a tough time by the Turf Moor crowd and moved on loan to Chesterfield in January 1972. The following month, he was signed by Bill Dodgin at Fulham, for a £25,000 fee. His displays helped keep the club in the Second Division and he rarely missed a match until a nasty injury in November 1976. He then fell out with new manager Bobby Campbell and was transferred to Hereford United in September 1977. This revived his career, and in July 1978 he moved to Portsmouth whom he helped to win promotion to Division Three in 1979-80. He played for Edmonton Drillers for the 1982 season, then retired from playing. Today, he runs his own business in Miami.

Bobby Robson

One of the great names in Fulham's post-war history, Bobby Robson started his career at the Cottage as an inside right, signing in October 1950 from Langley Park Juniors. He later formed a brilliant inside trio with Beddy Jezzard and Johnny Haynes, but in March 1956, Bobby moved to West Brom for £25,000. At the Hawthorns, he switched to wing-half, and won 20 England caps, mostly in midfield where he linked up again with Haynes. Robson returned to the Cottage in August 1962, playing in a more defensive role. He was a steadying influence at the back, and a competitive tackler whose distribution set up many attacks. He retired in May 1967 to become manager of Vancouver Royals, but returned to England to manage Fulham in January 1967. With Fulham plummeting towards the Third Division, he was sacked 11 months later, but his managerial career was revived by Ipswich Town in January 1969, where he stayed in charge for 13 years. Ipswich won the F.A. Cup in 1978, the UEFA Cup in 1981 and were also runners-up in the First Division that season. He became England manager in July 1982, and took them to the semi-finals of the 1990 World Cup. He then accepted the manager's job at PSV Eindhoven, who became Dutch champions during both his seasons at the club. In May 1992, he became the manager at Sporting Lisbon.

John Mitchell

With his two goals in the Cup semi-final matches against Birmingham in 1975, John Mitchell has ensured his place in Fulham's history. He joined the club for a mere £3,000 in February 1972 from St. Albans City. He broke through into the first team the following season, but inconsistency and injuries restricted his appearances. Fortunately, he got back into the side during the epic Cup run and struck his best form. For the next three seasons, he was the Cottagers' most reliable striker, forming a particularly effective partnership for a while with Teddy Maybank. Mitch was immensely popular with the Fulham supporters, and he was greatly missed when he moved to Millwall in the 1978 close season. Injuries ended his career at the age of 30, since when he has become as big a success in business as he was in Fulham's attack.

271

John Lacy

A tall, dominating centre-half, John Lacy completed his education before becoming a professional footballer. Gaining a BSc in Economics at the London School of Economics, Lacy played for Marine and Kingstonian before signing for Fulham in June 1971. He developed an excellent partnership with Bobby Moore in the side which reached the F.A. Cup final in 1975. Not renowned for his pace, it was his command in the air that made him a very necessary presence in the Fulham back four until he moved up into the First Division with Spurs, whom he joined in July 1978 for a £200,000 fee. After 133 appearances for Spurs, he moved to Crystal Palace in August 1983, and later played for Stenungsund of Gothenburg and St. Albans before becoming player-assistant manager at Wivenhoe in August 1988. He was also player-manager of St. Albans for a while in season 1987-88, but retired from playing in May 1991.

Eddie Lowe

Eddie Lowe was a tenacious tackler and an excellent defender whose skill was highly regarded by all his colleagues. At one time he was on amateur forms with Millwall and played for Finchley. In September 1945, he signed for Aston Villa and gained three caps for England. He moved to Fulham in May 1950 for a £10,000 fee with his brother Reg, and went on to make 511 appearances for the club. He was unlucky never to be capped whilst at the Cottage. Lowe played at left-half, full-back and centre-half for Fulham, helping them into the First Division in 1959 and playing a major role in the F.A. Cup run of 1962. After a sentimental send-off from the Cottage in May 1963, he became player-manager of Notts County, but struggled for success. He left Meadow Lane in April 1965, scouted for Plymouth Argyle for a while, and now lives in the Nottingham area.

Kevin Lock

A defender with a left foot as consistently accurate
as Steve Davis' snooker cue, Kevin Lock played
one of the best games of his life in the 1975 Cup
final, but unfortunately for Fulham, he was
playing for West Ham at the time. Signed by the
Hammers as the long-term replacement for Bobby
Moore, Lock eventually followed the former
England skipper to the Cottage in May 1978. At
wing-half, full-back or centre-half, his play was
stylish and unhurried, and his distribution
immaculate. Kevin was a superb penalty taker,
scoring twice against Liverpool in the 1983 League
Cup. By then, he was becoming injury prone and
he left Fulham in the summer of 1985 for
Southend. He was an integral part of the coaching
team which lifted the Shrimpers from the Fourth
to the Second Division in the late 1980s.

Alan Slough

Whether at full-back or in midfield, Alan Slough
could be relied on to give a thoroughly professional
performance. His versatility and 100% commitment
made him a vital member of the side for four seasons
between 1973 and 1977. He started at Luton in May
1965, and it was his former Kenilworth Road
manager, Alec Stock, who invested £45,000 to bring
him to the Cottage in August 1973. The value of his
contribution was never more apparent than during
the 1975 Cup run, when he also scored some vital
goals. Alan was the natural choice as Alan Mullery's
successor as captain in 1976, but he had just one
season in the role. The following summer he went to
Peterborough (where he got a hat-trick of penalties in
a match against Chester) and later had spells with
Millwall, Torquay, Weymouth, Yeovil and
Minehead.

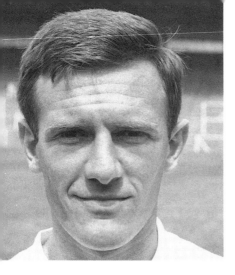

Johnny Key

Johnny Key signed for Fulham in May 1956. He was an old-fashioned winger who could take on his opponent and cross accurately. He made his debut in a Cup tie against Yeovil in January 1958, and scored, but it was several years before he established himself in the team. Key was unlucky that he had to compete with Graham Leggat and Tosh Chamberlain for one of the wing berths. His best game for Fulham was probably against Spurs in January 1965 in which he scored two goals in an excellent 4-1 win. At the end of the 1965-66 season, he was part of manager Vic Buckingham's over-zealous clear-out. Snapped up by his former team-mate Jimmy Hill, then the Coventry manager, Key showed he still had much to offer by helping the Sky Blues to promotion the next season. He finished his career at Orient in 1968-69, and today works as a taxi driver, preferring tennis as his main sporting interest.

Reg Matthewson

Small for a centre-half, but good in the air and steady on the ground, Reg was a very effective organiser in defence. He made his debut for his first club, Sheffield United, at the Cottage in March 1962, but was given the run-around by Maurice Cook, who scored a hat-trick. After 148 League appearances for the Blades, Matthewson moved to the Cottage in February 1968 for a fee of £30,000. Within 15 months, Fulham had sunk from the First to the Third Division, but Reg played an important role when the Cottagers clinched promotion back to Division Two in 1971. There was great celebration when he scored his one and only goal for Fulham in February 1971 against Torquay. He lost his place in the first team with the arrival of Paul Went, and although he played for and coached the reserves for a while, he wanted first-team soccer, and he moved to Chester in January in 1973. He retired from playing in 1976 to coach Wrexham. He was player-coach of Bangor City from 1978 to 1980, then assistant manager and coach with Shrewsbury Town, before leaving the game in 1981.

John Dempsey

A tall and dominating defender, John Dempsey joined Fulham as an apprentice in October 1962. Primarily a centre-half, he also had a spell at centre-forward, and scored a hat-trick against Northampton Town in the League Cup. It was a surprise when, in 1969, he was transferred to Chelsea for £70,000, signed by Blues manager Dave Sexton who had been coach at the Cottage when John first got into the team. But the move proved successful for him. With the Cottagers sinking into the Third Division, John was gaining F.A. Cup and European Cup winners medals with Chelsea, and also played in their League Cup Final side of 1972. He eventually moved to the States to play for Philadelphia Furies from March 1979. In 1981, he took over as the manager of Maidenhead, and later had spells in charge of Dundalk and Egham Town. He currently works with the physically handicapped in Edgware.

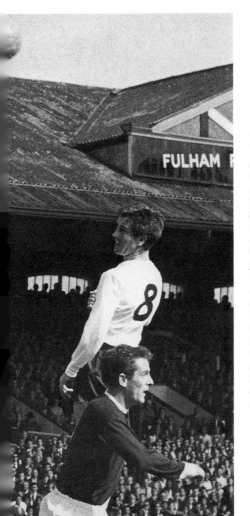

Brian 'Pat' O'Connell

A home-grown youngster who emerged as Fulham won a place in Division One, Brian O'Connell was to prove a loyal and versatile player for seven seasons. He signed as a junior in 1956 and made his debut in December 1958, from which time he was a regular member of the first-team squad until he left for Crystal Palace in July 1966. Most of his matches were at inside-forward or on the wing, but he also turned out at left-back with credit. The highlight of his Fulham career was a semi-final appearance in the Cup in 1962. Crystal Palace was his last League club, but he was still playing non-League football as late as 1975, appearing in the F.A. Vase final as Epsom and Ewell's player-manager.

Jimmy Dunne

Jimmy Dunne started his career in Ireland with Shelbourne before moving to Millwall in February 1966. After failing to make the grade at the Den, he moved to Torquay United in July 1967. He signed for Fulham in July 1970 for £15,000 and helped to tighten up the defence, leading to promotion at the end of his first season. He was capped by the Republic of Ireland in 1971 against Austria. An under-rated player and an extrovert personality, Jimmy was an excellent tackler and also had good passing ability. He did not see much future for himself at the Cottage after the arrival of Bobby Moore and decided to emigrate to South Africa to play for Durban City in the summer of 1974. He soon became home-sick and went back to Fulham in October 1975, but was unable to get into the first team again. In April he returned to Torquay United, and retired from playing in 1979.

Sean O'Driscoll

When Sean O'Driscoll signed for Fulham from Alvechurch in November 1979, Fulham paid the then sizeable fee of £12,000 to the non-League club. It was to prove money well spent, for he went on to become a very effective but under-rated member of the 1981-82 promotion team. 'Noisey', as he was nicknamed (because of his quiet manner) by Les Strong, made his debut in the struggling side which was relegated in 1980. He came to the fore, however, during Malcolm Macdonald's tenure, playing wide on the right. His surges down the wing set up many chances for colleagues, though he was also a lethal finisher himself. His displays won him international recognition for the Republic of Ireland, and it was a bad day's business for Fulham when he was sold to Bournemouth in 1984.

John Cutbush

A skilful right-back, the highlight of John Cutbush's career was playing for Fulham in the 1975 Cup final. His father Dennis was a petty officer in the Royal Navy, and had been an amateur international for England. He was stationed out in Malta when John was born in June 1949. John signed professional forms for Spurs in September 1966 after playing for Kent Schools, but never made the grade as a midfield player, and joined Fulham on a free transfer in August 1972. He was soon a first-team regular and developed into an indomitable and staunch defender. He moved to Sheffield United in March 1977, but was released after the club plunged into the Fourth Division in 1981. He played for Wichita Wings in America in 1979, but later returned to settle in the Sheffield area.

Bobby Moore

Bobby Moore was still a wonderful player when he came to the Cottage near the end of his career. A cool and sophisticated player, Bobby had a peerless record which included captaining England to a World Cup victory in 1966 and gaining 108 caps for his country. He joined West Ham in June 1958 and skippered the side to an F.A. Cup final victory in 1964 and a European Cup Winners Cup victory in 1965. Bobby was voted Footballer of the Year in 1964 and won Football League, Under-23 and Youth honours at Upton Park. After 642 games and 27 goals for the Hammers, he moved to Fulham in March 1974 for a £20,000 fee. He was inspirational as Fulham marched to Wembley in 1975. He left the Cottage in May 1977, and later played for San Antonio Thunder and Seattle Sounders in the N.A.S.L., and was player-coach at Herning of Denmark. He managed Oxford City and Eastern A.A. (Hong Kong), and then Southend United from February 1984 until April 1986, eventually becoming a director of the club.

Roger Brown

A tall, commanding and very brave central defender, Roger Brown won the hearts of Fulham supporters with his many outstanding displays. A late starter in professional football, having failed to make the grade as an apprentice with Walsall, he was working as a production manager in an engineering firm when he was signed by Bournemouth from A.P. Leamington in February 1978 for £5,000 at the age of 25. After some impressive performances for them, he was signed by First Division Norwich in July 1979, and moved to Fulham the following March for £100,000. He played a vital part in the club's promotion season in 1981-82 and scored 12 goals, a record for a defender in a season for Fulham. After losing his place at the start of 1983-84, Roger moved back to Bournemouth in December 1983. Later he was player-coach at Weymouth before becoming the manager of Colchester United from November 1987 until October 1988.

Viv Busby

Viv Busby was a much-travelled striker who played for seven other Football League clubs besides Fulham. Nevertheless, his contribution to the 1975 Cup run, especially his two goals at Everton, ensures his place in the club's history. In 1969, he was a trialist at Fulham, but when he did not make the grade he went first to Wycombe and then Luton and Newcastle, before his old Luton boss Alec Stock brought him to the Cottage in August 1973. He was a striker, but a clever ball player rather than a battering-ram, and he was a steady rather than a prolific scorer. After leaving Fulham in 1976, he played for Norwich, Stoke, Sheffield United, Blackburn and York, where he went into management with team-mate Denis Smith.

Robert Wilson

An attacking midfield player who came through the Fulham youth scheme, Robert Wilson was a key member of the 1981-82 promotion side. Although lacking a little in pace, he was fiercely competitive and orchestrated many intricate close-passing moves. He was also adept at making late runs into the penalty area and was the scorer of some vital goals. He had joined Fulham as an apprentice in July 1977, and he signed professional two years later. A turning-point in Wilson's first stay at the Cottage was a domestic accident, a gas leak which nearly ended in tragedy. After spells with Millwall and Luton, he returned to Fulham for a second, shorter, and less successful spell in September 1987, and later played for Rotherham and Huddersfield.

Ray Lewington

A loyal club servant, Lewington first joined Fulham towards the end of the relegation season of 1979-80. A hard-working ball winner in midfield, he had started with Chelsea in 1974, and had spells with Vancouver Whitecaps and Wimbledon before signing for Fulham. He arrived too late to help the club avoid relegation, but was an influential player in the 1981-82 promotion success. Lewington succeeded Roger Brown as captain, but in 1985 he moved to Sheffield United. He was back at the Cottage 12 months later, appointed by new owners Marler Estates to replace Ray Harford as manager. Since then, he has continued with Fulham as manager, chief coach or caretaker manager.

John Beck

In recent years, John Beck has made a name for himself in football management with Cambridge United. Since taking control at the Abbey Stadium in January 1990, he has steered the club from the Fourth Division to the Second Division promotion play-offs. Beck started his career as a professional with QPR before moving to Coventry in June 1976 and then to Fulham just over two years later. An excellent crosser of a ball and dangerous with free-kicks, Beck was a cultured midfield playmaker whose style was almost the antithesis of his approach as a manager. A regular at Fulham for over four years, he captained the team on numerous occasions. Bobby Campbell's departure signalled the end of his tenure at the Cottage, and he eventually moved on to Bournemouth in February 1983, the first of four Fulham players to find their way to Dean Court.

Bobby Keetch

Bobby Keetch was an uncompromising and tough-tackling centre-half who was feared by opposing players and hugely popular with Fulham supporters. He joined the club in April 1959 after playing for West Ham Juniors, and made his debut in a League Cup tie against Sheffield United in September 1961. He established himself as the regular centre-half in 1963-64. He was heart-broken when released on a free transfer by manager Vic Buckingham in May 1966. He left football, but later that year QPR manager Alec Stock persuaded him to play again. He made 51 League appearances for Rangers before retiring from the game in 1969 at the young age of 27, having helped them rise from the Third to the First Division. Outside football, Bobby had a sophisticated lifestyle and was heavily involved in the art and antique world. Today, he still works in that industry and travels the world as an importer. He is well known for his love of the 'good life'.

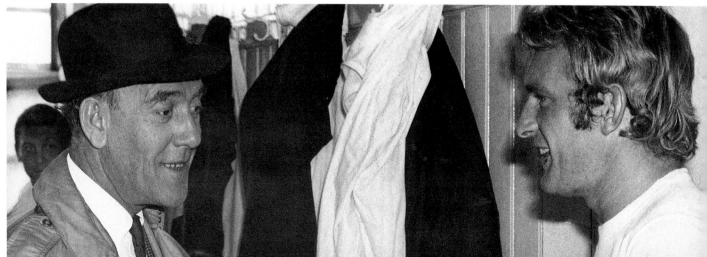

Richard Money

Although the move occurred more than 12 years ago, the £333,333 fee Fulham received from Liverpool for Richard Money in April 1980 remains a club record. This was another example of manager Bobby Campbell's shrewdness in the transfer market, for Money had been signed from Scunthorpe for just £50,000 in December 1977. He made an immediate impact at the Cottage, and displayed versatility, performing well in either defence or midfield. When the team struggled in 1979-80, however, his form appeared to suffer, and his move was not unexpected. But his stay at Anfield was brief, for 18 months later he had an extended loan period with Derby before signing for Luton in April 1982. He later went to Portsmouth, but a serious injury cut short his career. In 1985, Richard was back at Scunthorpe as player-coach. More recently, he was youth team coach at Aston Villa.

Terry Bullivant

A destroyer and ball-winner in midfield, Terry Bullivant signed professional for Fulham in May 1974, having been with the club since his schooldays. He broke through into the first team in 1977 and his tenacity, enthusiasm and high-energy performances caught the eye. It was nevertheless a surprise when, in November 1979, Villa manager Ron Saunders paid nearly a quarter of a million pounds for him. Terry's opportunities at Villa Park were limited, however, and in the summer of 1982 he was back in London, with Charlton. He later moved on to Brentford, Reading, and Maidstone before returning to the Cottage in 1987. Initially a part-time coach and reserve team player, Terry became youth team manager, a role he combined with taxi driving.

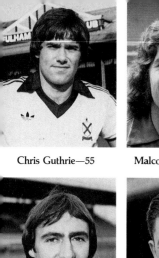
Chris Guthrie—55

Malcolm Webster—104

Ray Evans—89

Bill Dodgin—77

The Players
...continued

Peter Kitchen—23

Joe Stapleton—26

Peter Marinello—32

Mark Pearson—66

Ian Seymour—75

Paul Went—6

Alan Warboys—21

John Gilchrist—27

Jackie Henderson—56

George Johnston—42

George Best—47

Brian Nicholls—

Ernie Howe—77

Gary Peters—72

Rodney Marsh—90

Jimmy Hill—82

Terry Parmenter—22

Reg Stratton—

Ray Houghton—54

John Ryan—55

Stan Horne—87

Dave Clement—20

John Margerrison—79

Allan Clarke—

Ronnie Goodlass—27

John Fraser—66

Teddy Maybank—50

Vic Halom—82

Dai Edwards—21

Derek Lampe—

During the production of this book, these two pages became known as the Rogues' Gallery, which is quite unfair, of course. A more elegant collection of footballers you would be unlikely to find.

The Fulham men shown here are all those players who made at least 20 first-team appearances during the period covered by this book. (Apart, that is, from the top 40 players highlighted on previous pages.) Following each player's name is the number of first-team appearances he made. The players are in random order.

Thank you, gentlemen, for contributing to Fulham's Golden Years.

Roy Bentley—95

Cliff Jones—26

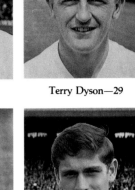
Terry Dyson—29

John Dowie—50

Jack McClelland—57

Tosh Chamberlain—108

Dean Coney—104

Jeff Hopkins—98

Dave Metchick—56

Dale Tempest—20

John Evanson—107

Bobby Howfield—31

Brian Greenaway—94

John Richardson—80

Jim Stannard—22

Dave Roberts—25

Frank Large—28

Paul Parker—34

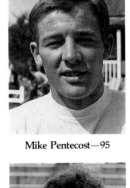
Robin Lawler—63

Geoff Banton—45

John Conway—45

Roger Cross—46

John Doherty—40

Wilf Tranter—25

Mike Pentecost—95

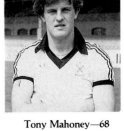
Peter O'Sullivan—55

Ken Hewkins—26

Joe Gilroy—28

Barry Mealand—35

Dave Moreline—82

Steve Hatter—32

Tony Mahoney—68

Mike Johnson—27

THE GROUND

F ulham's famous ground on the banks of the Thames is in fact the club's ninth location. For 17 years at the start of its history, the club wandered around temporary grounds before settling at its present Craven Cottage site nearly 100 years ago. The first match was played there in October 1896. The present Stevenage Road stand and the club's offices—the Craven Cottage—were designed by Archibald Leitch and were opened in 1905. The ground is renowned for its homely, friendly atmosphere; it has a special place in the affection of Fulham fans, and, indeed, of football fans everywhere.

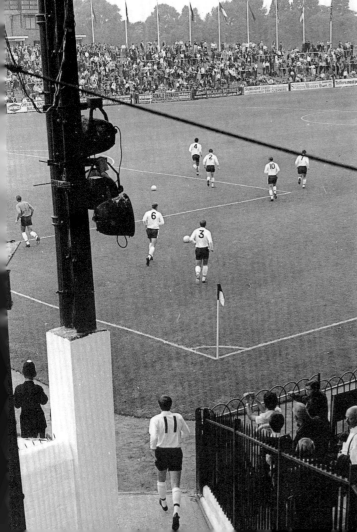

ASHWATER
PUBLISHING